The
GREAT GRETZKY
Yearbook II

**The Greatest Single Season
In Hockey History**

The GREAT GRETZKY
Yearbook II

The Greatest Single Season In Hockey History

by
TERRY JONES

PUBLISHED BY *General* PAPERBACKS

A Division of General Publishing Co. Limited
Toronto, Canada

Published in 1982 by
General Paperbacks,
A Division of General Publishing Co. Limited,
30 Lesmill Road,
Toronto, Canada
M3B 2T6

Canadian Cataloguing in Publication Data
   Jones, Terry.
     The great Gretzky yearbook II
   ISBN 0-7736-7042-4
   1. Gretzky, Wayne, 1961–   2. Hockey players–
   Canada–Biography. I. Title.
   GV848.5.G78J67   796.96′2′0924   C82-095054-8

Cover photograph by Brian Gavriloff, *Edmonton Journal*.
Used by permission.

Book design by **Joe Stevens**

Printed and bound in Canada

To my son, Shane

And to every father who has a sporting idol
and every father's son in search of one.

About the Author

Terry Jones, author of the original edition of *The Great Gretzky* in 1980, is the sports columnist of the *Edmonton Sun*.

Jones, who has also written two *Canadian Pro Football* books and co-authored *Decade of Excellence*, the story of the Edmonton Eskimos of the '70s, joined the staff of the *Edmonton Journal* in 1967. In 1972, he won a national award for sportswriting and became the *Journal's* sports columnist in 1976. He joined the *Edmonton Sun* in June of 1982.

A native of Lacombe, Alberta, Jones began his career in journalism with the weekly *Lacombe Globe* when he was in junior high school. He joined the staff of the *Red Deer Advocate* on a part-time/full-time basis while still in high school and became a member of the *Journal's* sports staff on graduation.

Jones, who has won the Edmonton Press Club award for sportswriting each time it has been offered, covered the Edmonton Oilers in the World Hockey Association and the Edmonton Eskimos of the Canadian Football League as a beat reporter prior to becoming the *Journal's* sports columnist.

A sportswriter who has covered such events as the Grey Cup, the Super Bowl, the Stanley Cup, Canada Cup, NHL Challenge Cup, World Series, Indianapolis 500, Olympic Games, Commonwealth Games, The World Figure Skating Championships, U.S. PGA and Bing Crosby golf tournaments, the Preakness, Boston Marathon and many others, also does twice-daily sports commentary shows on Edmonton radio station CHQT.

Terry and his wife, Linda, live with their son Shane and twin daughters Trina and Nicole in Sherwood Park, Alberta.

Acknowledgments

Despite the gentle elbow in his direction in this book, I want to express my appreciation to Jim Proudfoot of the *Toronto Star*, for it was at his suggestion that I undertook this project.

A very special vote of thanks to Walter Gretzky for his kind cooperation.

My sincere gratitude, as well, to Cam Cole of the *Edmonton Journal* for his efforts beyond the call of duty in the editing of the copy. And to the many sportswriters—including Dick Chubey, Jim Matheson, Jim Coleman, Ted Beare, Dick Denny, Tony Fitz-Gerald, and Doug Milroy—my appreciation for their cooperation.

I'd also like to express appreciation to Mike Griffin and Benny Ercolani of the National Hockey League, Ron Andrews, and to amateur statistician Tom Barrett for their assistance in assembling the statistical section.

Special thanks to Colorfast and photographer Bob Peterson and Brian Gavriloff, *Edmonton Journal* photographer, who shot the majority of the color pictures for the book.

But most of all, to my wife Linda and our three children many, many thanks for all the patience and all the understanding.

T.J.

A young Wayne Gretzky, ten going on eleven, laces up his skates
(THE GLOBE AND MAIL)

1

When the Kid was Really a Kid

The first goal Wayne Gretzky ever scored was during Hockey Night in Canning.

He beat his grandmother on the glove side.

His grandmother lived in Canning, Ont., and every Saturday night Walter and Phyllis Gretzky took their young son to visit his grandmother. While Walter watched Hockey Night in Canada on television, little Wayne Douglas Gretzky would take off his shoes and slide on stocking feet on the well-polished pine living-room floor.

"He'd stride and pretend he was skating like the players on television," remembers his dad. "His grandmother bought him one of those little hockey sticks that you find in souvenir stands. And he'd have that stick and a little ball. His grandmother would sit in her big chair and she'd be his goaltender.

"By the end of the evening, she'd have bruised legs from getting hit with his little souvenir hockey stick."

Mrs. Mary Gretzky, his grandmother, was convinced that young Wayne would one day grow up to be another Frank Mahovlich, her favorite hockey player.

Sixteen years later, The Kid would bring her a picture of himself posing with his World Hockey Association All-Star team-mate, Gordie Howe. He autographed the picture with the message: "Sorry it's not Frank, grandma, but Gordie will have to do."

It was about 70 metres behind his grandmother's house, on the Nith River, that young Wayne, at age two, would take his first strides on skates. While he skated, his father, an amateur photographer, captured what someday should be a Hockey Hall of Fame movie of his son.

His grandmother was no longer playing goal, and, as time passed, she learned to remain at a safe distance.

"Wayne always had a hockey stick in his hands," recalls Walter. "I'll never forget the time Wayne's grandfather had just replaced a window in his house that Wayne had broken with a shot. My dad had just completed the task of putting a new window in and he was standing back admiring his work when—smash!—Wayne took another shot at the side of his house and broke the window again. I can still see his grandfather chasing him with a hockey stick while his grand-

January 1968 on the backyard rink,
six going on seven
(WALTER GRETZKY)

mother stood back and laughed her head off.

"His grandfather ended up putting a board in front of the window every time he figured we'd be coming over."

"Wayne kept us in the poorhouse repairing windows," remembers his mother, Phyllis.

The neighbor across the street from the modest house at 42 Veradi in Brantford, Ont., where Walter and Phyllis Gretzky live to this day, used to call the Ontario Provincial Police to report their son.

"Wayne always played ball hockey in front of the house and when the ball rolled across the road to her lawn, she'd call the police. The woman across the road was always scared to death that a car would hit him," Phyllis also recalls.

No ordinary young man

Little Wayne Gretzky was never an ordinary lad.

Walter Gretzky describes his son, for all the years he lived at home, as being "quiet and backward." That isn't the Wayne of today. But he was bashful and so shy it was pathetic. He kept everything to himself. It wasn't until he had to move away from home and go to Toronto that he came out of his shell.

"One thing I noticed about Wayne when he was a young boy is that he never played with toys," remembers his dad. "He had all the toys any kid would want, but he'd never play with them. But give him a hockey stick or a lacrosse stick or a baseball bat, it didn't matter, and he'd be in his glory. He'd never get bored.

"I remember many times that other kids would come over in the afternoon and ask if Wayne wanted to go to

10

a show with them. Wayne never cared about going. His friends would go to the show and he'd stay home, by himself, firing a ball at the wall until he'd knock the bricks out. Some days it would be 90 degrees out and he'd be out there firing the ball against the wall."

The place where Wayne Gretzky was happiest as a kid was the backyard at 42 Veradi in winter.

From the time Wayne was three, every year, Walter Gretzky would wait until the ground froze, cut the grass very short, and then get out the lawn sprinkler — which made for the most even flood — and turn the backyard, from fence to fence, into a 60' x 40' hockey rink.

His father had definite ideas

Walter Gretzky says he didn't push his kids into hockey, but he admits they were surrounded with the environment. And Wayne's father had some definite ideas about things.

"I believe in sport," said his dad, who for 25 years has worked for Bell Telephone in Brantford. "I believe that a kid who participates in sport ends up much more mature and much brighter than kids who don't. And they learn that if you want something, you have to work for it."

If there's one thing Walter Gretzky taught his son that he believes has shown up in his game, it's patience.

"Patience is one of his most underrated assets. He's like a vulture, the way he waits for somebody to make a mistake. When the other team doesn't make many mistakes, Wayne isn't that noticeable."

There were other things Walter believes contributed to the skills of his eldest son.

"I don't think I pushed any of the kids into sport. But I told them when they decided to go into a sport, I believed they shouldn't give it a half effort. Some people may say that's pushing. But I believe when you go into sport, you have to try to do the best you can all the time. I don't believe in the minor hockey philosophy that the kids should just be sent out to go have fun. To me, that's ridiculous. If the boy is sent out to do the best he can do, and he does it, he's going to be happy."

Track and field, Walter Gretzky believes, ought not to be overlooked in trying to determine just what it is that makes Wayne great.

"All my kids have participated in track and field and I think it provides something special for an athlete," said Walter, whose daughter Kim appeared to be on her way to national prominence in the sport when she slipped on a patch of ice and badly damaged her ankle.

"Track and field teaches you that you only get out what you put in. You learn how to excel within yourself. It builds self-discipline and it builds confidence. Nobody else is going to help you, only you."

Stereotype Canadian hockey dream?

It was the stereotype "Canadian dream." Backyard rink. Scrubs-on-skates to stardom. Except most of the time there were pylons on the backyard rink — and that, some would say, is closer to the stereotype "Soviet dream."

Fifteen years ago, pylons were an unusual sight on a Canadian ice surface.

"I used to get a kick out of reading

the stories about the European way of teaching hockey," Wayne remembered of the press surrounding the '72 Canada-Russia Summit Series. "My dad was teaching me that way when I was six."

Walter says he wasn't teaching anything in particular the Soviets did.

"But I guess we did a lot of things that weren't being done in Canadian minor hockey. You have to remember that in those times we didn't stress a lot of things we do now. All I was trying to do was stick to common sense."

The pylons?

"Possession is nine-tenths of the law," said Walter Gretzky. "The pylons work wonders for puck possession. Pylons and practice make perfect. The amazing thing, though, was that Wayne never got bored with skating around those pylons."

It wasn't always Wayne alone in the backyard, of course.

All the guys from the Nadrofsky Steelers used to come over. There were boys like Greg Stefan, Jimmy Burton and Lenny Hachborn. That was half a lifetime ago.

When Wayne Gretzky was en route to winning the scoring championship in the National Hockey League — breaking records many thought would never be broken — when Wayne was on his way to winning a second straight Hart Trophy as the Most Valuable Player in the NHL, the kids from half a lifetime ago were in junior hockey.

Greg Stefan was a goalie with the Oshawa Generals, Jimmy Burton a defenceman with the Windsor Spitfires, and Lenny Hachborn was with the Brantford Alexanders.

"We'd play in that backyard rink all day," said Stefan. "Eight hours at a time. There was a spotlight on it. We'd even play at night. There were hockey nets all around the yard, regardless of what time of the year it was. And all the guys on the team would go over there. We all hung around him when we were kids. He was a super guy. He didn't brag. And he's still that way."

"At times it's hard for me to believe we were the same age and I used to play with him," says Jimmy Burton. "He's already done just about everything there is to do in the NHL."

"I guess," said Stefan, "we've been friends and at the same time idolized him ever since we were kids."

They called him a 'hot dog'

While they'd certainly trade places with Wayne now, the kids who grew up with him, the kids who know how it was, wouldn't have wanted to, then.

"Half the time we felt sorry for him," said Lenny Hachborn, who scored between 150 and 160 goals playing with Gretzky on the Nadrofsky Steelers in 1971-72. "Back then, no, I wouldn't have traded places with him. He had all that pressure. Everybody was always out for him, slashing him. Even at that age. And there were all the problems with the parents who were jealous of how good he was. Most of the parents resented him. Now they're all bragging that their kids once played on the same team as Wayne Gretzky."

Jimmy Burton said it was never the kids.

"I felt sorry for him too. He was always picked on. And labelled a 'hot dog'. He was never a 'hot dog'. He was so modest, it was unbelievable. I know the three of us were never jealous of him. I don't think any of the other kids were either. I think we *depended* on him more than we were jealous of him."

"He wasn't a hog with the puck,"

says Stefan. "He set up plays like you wouldn't believe."

The three of them vividly remember watching Wayne, who scored an incredible 378 goals in 1971-72, cry after games.

"When we lost, he felt he was to blame," said Burton. "When he cried, nobody would say anything. Some of the other guys would cry too."

Send, don't take your boy to the rink

It wasn't easy, half a lifetime ago, for Wayne Gretzky.

"We, as parents, really get involved," said his father, Walter Gretzky, looking back on those days on the occasion of Wayne's eighteenth birthday, and trying to explain to Edmonton Oiler fans what it had been like for his son. "I do. I'm like everyone else. We lost sight of the fact it has to be fun for the kids."

Phyllis Gretzky still takes her kids to the rink. "But I learned a long time ago to sit by myself," she said.

Walter Gretzky doesn't talk about the harrassment his eldest son had to endure without first pointing out that "it was a small minority" and that "most of the people in Brantford were just super."

But that small minority. . .

"When I was coach, I could never take Wayne aside for even a minute without parents saying I was favoring him," says Walter Gretzky. "So I would spend the time with Wayne in the backyard."

After Wayne scored 378 goals when he was ten, going on eleven, his friends weren't the only ones feeling sorry for him.

"The fun left the game for him," said his dad.

"When I was twelve," Wayne admitted, "it ran through my mind. I thought of quitting."

At the age of fourteen, he left Brantford. Many of the reports, at the time, suggested it was because he wanted better competition so he could become a better hockey player.

"That was completely false," said Wayne. "The league I went to play in wasn't really any better than the league I could have played in at home. I just had to get away from the people. I didn't need it any more. It was really sickening. It really got to me."

"Many a time I saw him crying," remembers Walter Gretzky. "Some of the parents called him a 'puck hog' and a 'one-man team' when they won and blamed him when they lost."

"That's why I sit by myself now," says Phyllis Gretzky. "This way, I keep my friends."

There are dozens of examples of how it was.

Walter Gretzky remembers the day his team won the final game of a tournament 4-3.

"When Wayne came into the hallway outside of the dressing room, I asked him if he wanted a Coke. He said no. Kids always want a Coke. I asked him how come he didn't want one. He wouldn't answer. He just wanted to go. His eyes were red.

"You know what his coach told him after the game? His coach said to him, 'Do you have to be such a damn "hot dog" out there?' Wayne was never a 'hot dog'."

Wayne remembers a game he lost.

"It was the year I scored 378 goals. We lost a tournament final 3-2. I scored both of our goals. But we played our back-up netminder, who really wasn't very good. They had five shots on goal and scored on three."

It wasn't losing because of a kid who wasn't very good that hurt Wayne.

"The father of the back-up goaltender who played for us in that final game, came up to me after it was over and really lit into me. He blamed me for losing. I guess I should have laughed it off. But at that age, it really hurt."

Walter Gretzky, despite the fact Wayne's younger brothers have proven to have the same kind of magic touch, says the parents treat his other kids the way he wished they'd treated Wayne.

"I have to admit, I'm getting more enjoyment out of watching my other boys play hockey than I did with Wayne," he confessed.

The 'novice' who wasn't

Wayne scored his first goal—his only goal of the season—when he was five, going on six. At the time he was playing against players who were as old as nine and ten. Walter Gretzky, who fixes teletype machines for Bell Telephone, is an amateur photographer and he managed to snap a stop-action shot of Wayne's first goal. That was in 1967-68.

Wayne's dad kept the stats every season.

When he was six, going on seven, Wayne scored twenty-seven goals.

The year after that, he scored 104.

In 1970-71, Wayne scored 196.

And then, the BIG year. Three hundred and seventy-eight goals.

"That was his last year in novice," said his coach, and uncle, Bob Hockin. "He should have been playing pee wee hockey then. It was just about the only year he played with boys his own age."

Hockin remembers it all like yesterday. The good and the bad.

"If we were losing, having a bad time of it, the parents were wondering why Wayne wasn't doing this and wasn't doing that. When we were up 8-1 or something, they figured he should be sitting on the bench most of the game so their kids could be on the ice more than he was. My feeling was that if he won games for us by himself one night, he should at least be able to play a regular shift the next night."

Not that there was anything "regular" about a Gretzky shift.

"He played defence most of the time that year," remembers Hockin. "Until, of course, the puck was dropped."

They loved to see him fail

"I remember one tournament we entered in Hespeler," tells Hockin. "Wayne scored fifty goals in six games. Almost every time he got the puck, he took it and went and scored with it. There really isn't any other way to describe the goals.

"But just as vividly, I remember the times when one of our kids hadn't scored a goal for a long time and Wayne would go through the whole team and then position himself by the side of the net. Instead of scoring himself, he'd position himself in such a way that he could feed the puck to the kid who hadn't scored a goal. He'd pass it to them all. The kids didn't have anything against him."

But the parents did.

"It was everybody," said Lenny Hachborn's mother, Lil.

"I felt sorry for him because of the way they'd boo him," she remembers. "They'd cheer if he was knocked down. You could see it, every parent wanted to be Mr. Gretzky. A lot of people were always complaining that the team was only entering all the tournaments because of Wayne. They couldn't seem to see that their kids were on the ice too. And getting tremendous experiences out of it. It was really tough on the Gretzky family, especially Phyllis."

Asked if she thinks Brantford deserves to have a black eye from it all, Mrs. Hachborn said, "Yes, I feel that way. Brantford is certainly proud of him now but, in many ways, Brantford hasn't had all that much to do with where he is now."

Most of that is water under the bridge to Wayne and his parents. The memories they, and everybody else, like to recall now are the good ones.

And it's difficult to bring up the name Wayne Gretzky anywhere in Southern Ontario without someone remembering a minor league hockey game they attended where he played.

Bob Wagner, who coached at that time in one of the largest minor hockey leagues in the Toronto area, remembers when the team his son played on had the experience of going up against Gretzky.

"My son played for the Cedar Hill Cougars in the Metro Toronto Hockey League," he said. "And the team was considered a club of young superstars. They'd never been beaten. The club goes down to Brantford to play against Wayne Gretzky's team and loses 6-0. One boy stopped the whole team. He scored four of the goals and assisted on two others. The next time we played Brantford it was in our backyard and it was a different story. Our team led 8-0 in the third period and this kid Gretzky brings them back to win 11-10."

The most dramatic memory Hockin has of Wayne involved his play in a tournament in Peterborough.

"We were playing Oshawa and we were down 5-0 in the third period and I was using Wayne all 60 minutes that game. Except in the third period, I

pulled him off the ice for thirty seconds. It was the only time he was off the ice in the whole game. I told him, 'Wayne, you can score enough by yourself to win this game'. And he went out and scored six straight goals and we won the game 6-5.

"When Wayne was nine, he played for two teams: The major novice team for me and the minor novice team, mostly made up of nine-year-olds, his regular team from the other years, for his dad. We had him signed to two cards. After that year they changed the rules so a kid couldn't do that

Wayne has a phenomenal year—378 goals in eighty-five games
(THE GLOBE AND MAIL)

again. Wayne was playing for me in the Silver Stick tournament in Welland and in another tournament in Hespeler. But by the end of the weekend, his dad figured it was too tough on him. He decided Wayne better not come back to play with my team for our last game.

"But Wayne wanted to play. He finally talked his dad into letting him. He didn't want to let my team down. I'll never forget when we got the phone call. My team was down 2-0. The news just went through the rink like a prairie fire. Wayne is on his way! My players said, 'Come on, we can hold them down until Wayne gets here'. And they did. Walter carried young Wayne in from the car and dropped him over the boards. And we won both tournaments.

(WALTER GRETZKY)

"It was a fantastic year, looking back on it, despite some of the things that happened.

"One night, I remember, we were playing a zone playoff game in Welland and a bunch of teenagers, some of them older brothers of players on the team we were playing against, decided that they were going to beat Wayne up. We had to get police protection at the rink and a police escort out of town."

The one game Lenny Hachborn loves to tell about was a game in Grimsby.

"He scored nine goals and added nine assists," said Lenny. "Eighteen points!"

"I think the most goals I ever scored in one game was eleven," Gretzky admitted at one of his frequent interviews at the ripe old age of sixteen.

In 1972-73, in major pee wee, Wayne scored 104 goals. And the following year, also in major pee wee, he scored 191.

Signing autographs at age ten

On April 10th, 1974, Wayne Gretzky reached a minor hockey milestone.

As the *Brantford Examiner* reported the following day: "Wayne Gretzky got the puck inside the Waterford blueline and let go with a slapshot. The Waterford goalie got a piece of the puck, but not enough to keep it from going into the net. Players rushed onto the ice and the game was held up for several minutes. Gretzky had scored his 1,000th career goal!"

"What would normally thrill a boy doesn't thrill Wayne anymore," Walter Gretzky was quoted as saying after that game. "But last night he was definitely thrilled."

The best memory the kids have from those days, is the year when they were pee wees and they got to go to the famed Quebec Winter Carnival in Quebec City.

"We only lost two or three games in the years we played with Wayne," remembers Greg Stefan, the goalie, who says he didn't get more than a dozen or so shots on goal per game.

"We had a lot of tournament wins. But there was nothing quite like the Winter Carnival trip. It was a wonderful experience for us. Wayne had received a lot of publicity. And we were used to having big crowds watch us play. But in Quebec City the papers were full of stuff about him before we even got there and there were photographers asking him to pose when we arrived. And the thing I'll never forget was that there were kids only a year or two younger than him, asking for his autograph.

"We played one game at 8:00 A.M. and the big coliseum there was packed. Everybody wanted to see him.

"He broke Guy Lafleur's record for the tournament."

Obviously, there were some comparisons made there with Lafleur. But mostly, people were calling him "The Next Bobby Orr." From the time he was six, he'd been called "The Next Bobby Orr."

But at the age of ten, when he was being followed around by a television network and major magazines such as *Sports Illustrated*, The Kid was making it perfectly clear that he had no desire to be the next Bobby Orr. He wanted to be the next Gordie Howe.

"Bobby Orr doesn't have any tricks," he was quoted as saying back then. "Not as many tricks as Gordie Howe. I like Gilbert Perreault better than I like Bobby Orr."

Gordie Howe was soon to begin to cross paths with Wayne Gretzky on a rather regular basis.

Wayne's second year of hockey, April 1969. He is second from the left in the first row.
(WALTER GRETZKY)

Wayne during his metro junior B season in Toronto
(THE GLOBE AND MAIL)

18

CHAPTER

2

"What Are You Trying to Do to My Son?"

Gretzky had played his last game in Brantford and was about to head to the Young Nationals where he'd play on the same team as Howe's son Murray. How he became a Toronto Young National is something of an involved story.

Sam McMaster was the man in the middle.

McMaster, the general manager of the Nats isn't sure when he first saw Wayne Gretzky play. But like Wayne's team-mates, he'll never forget the scene at the tournament in Quebec City.

"First thing in the morning and there were 13,000 people in a 10,000 seat stadium. The only place I could sit was in the aisle.

"I had gotten to know the Gretzky family over the years. I guess baseball had the most to do with it," he recalls of the sport which Wayne, to this day, maintains is his favorite.

"His dad, Walter, was helping schedule ball games and I phoned to schedule an exhibition game for my team. His dad wasn't home. And I started talking to Wayne.

"I asked him about his last year in bantam. He said it was lousy. He said the fans were all on his back. That his family was upset. And everybody was booing him. I told him if he wanted, he could come and stay with me and live in Toronto."

A few weeks later, McMaster received a call from Walter Gretzky.

"Walter was upset. He asked me what I was trying to do to his son," recalls McMaster.

"I said, 'What do you mean?'

"Walter said, 'He won't eat with us anymore!'"

Wayne had asked his dad if he could go live with McMaster in Toronto and his dad's first response was "No."

"I guess what finally convinced Walter that it was in the best interests of everybody was when Wayne asked him why he couldn't go live in Toronto and his dad told him that he was too young. Wayne asked how come he was too young, and his dad said he was worried that if he wasn't close to home, he might end up drinking or taking drugs.

"Apparently Wayne told his father, 'Dad, I can do that here. If you want I'll take you and show you where I can get booze and drugs'."

At that point, Walter Gretzky realized just how mature his young son had become.

"On August 1st," recalls McMaster, "I received a call from Wayne saying, 'I can come to Toronto'. I said, 'Good'. Then I had to find out if things were legal."

McMaster's first investigation left him convinced there would be no problem.

"I found no rule which prohibited it. And I went to the Brantford team and the president and secretary of the league gave me his release with no problem. They were 100 percent cooperative.

"He moved in with Bill Cornish on August 16th and he would live there and go to school and play hockey with our bantams. We put him under guardianship. But it wasn't because of anticipating any hockey problems.

It was for the purposes of schooling and taxes.

"He played an exhibition game and there was no problem, but then I got a phone call from the president of the Metro Toronto Hockey League. He said, 'There's going to be trouble'."

The Ontario Minor Hockey Association said Gretzky could not play because he had not received an interbranch transfer.

"Bill Glover of the Metro Toronto Hockey Association said I needed a release from the jurisdiction called Ontario Minor. And they said they weren't releasing him.

"Everybody was telling me it wasn't worth my trouble. Knowledgeable hockey men were telling me they'd watched Wayne in his final year in Brantford and they swore he was burned out, past his prime. They said he couldn't skate and that he'd never make it."

McMaster explained the situation to Wayne.

"I told him we could try to appeal it. Or he could go back to Brantford. He said he wanted to appeal it.

"The first thing we did was go to court to try to get an injunction against everybody. But the court ruled, and rightfully so I guess, that we must try all avenues of appeal within the hockey structure before they'd hear it.

"We took the appeal to the Ontario Minor Hockey Association in October to their annual meeting. And they turned us down on the grounds that Wayne was moving strictly to improve his hockey. They said there was no exact rule, but their decision was made on 'the spirit of the rule'. There was a lot of press over this thing and almost all of the opinion and comment was in favor of Wayne playing in Toronto."

But by this point Wayne had been out of hockey for five weeks. It was beginning to bug him.

"That's when I suggested Wayne go out and practice with the junior B team. Junior B came under different jurisdiction than bantam. It was legal for him to do that because now we were dealing with the Ontario Hockey Association. One day we were told, 'Yes, he could play.' The next day we were told, 'No he couldn't.' Then the day after that, 'Yes, he could' again.

"But everybody was laughing at us. Not only were there all those comments about Wayne being washed up at his age, but now they were saying we were going to hurt him. That we were doing the wrong thing for the boy."

After one practice with the junior B team, Wayne decided that, yes, he could play at that level.

He scored two goals in his first game.

"Wayne was happy. His family had come up for the game and they were happy," recalls McMaster. "And then at 2:00 A.M. I get a phone call from Walter. He told me 'They just suspended my boy'. The Ontario Minor Hockey Association had suspended Wayne for leaving without a release. He'd scored two goals and now everybody was mad. Walter worries a lot. But I told him: 'Walter, don't worry about it'."

This time they won. And Wayne Gretzky began his junior B hockey career.

"He was the Metro Junior B 'Rookie of the Year'," McMaster says matter-of-factly.

There was another boy involved in all the headlines with Gretzky that year. A kid by the name of Brian Rorabeck was in a similar situation. He continued the fight after Wayne

jumped up to junior B. The appeal finally ended up at a tribunal, the highest hockey court in the region. It voted to allow him to play. Wayne, it turned out, could have played bantam hockey later that year. But by then he was doing so well in junior B, he wondered why he'd intended to play bantam in the first place.

The Wayne Gretzky Era begins

The second season with the Toronto Young Nationals was the only year of the five years he was away from home prior to his twentieth birthday that Wayne would not win a 'Rookie of the Year' award, much less whatever version of the Hart and Lady Byng awards the leagues had to offer.

"But that second year with us," remembers Sam McMaster, "was the start of the Wayne Gretzky Era."

It wasn't until the playoffs started that the Gretzky Era started. But he scored seventy-three points in twenty-three games in the playoffs.

"And it almost didn't happen. We were tied with Stratford at two games each and we were very close to losing out in the first round of the best-of-five playoff series. With ten minutes to play in the fifth game, we were losing 5-1. With four minutes left we were leading 6-5. Wayne scored four goals and added one assist in that span. We ended up winning 7-6 and Wayne had scored five goals.

"I really believe if we had not won that game, Wayne wouldn't have been rated in the top 100 players going into the draft. People didn't want to believe. If he'd been out of the playoffs early, he wouldn't have been drafted high. As it turned out he was the third pick of the first round by Sault Ste. Marie."

McMaster has great memories of the Gretzky years in Toronto.

"I'll never forget his first goal in junior B. He went past the net. And all of a sudden the red light was on. I couldn't believe he scored from there. So I asked him, 'How did you score from there?' I'll never forget his answer as long as I live and I decided right then and there I'd never ask him about a goal again.

"He said, 'I shot it the only place it would go'.

"I mean it was a backhand over the goaltender's shoulder from the most incredible angle. And he viewed it as 'the only place it would go'."

Not only would Wayne get to meet Gordie Howe during these years, he'd meet a man by the name of Gus Badali.

"Murray Howe lived with Gus Badali," McMaster recalls. "Gus didn't know anything about Wayne. But he went to a few games when Murray was in the line-up and one day he asked me about talking to the Gretzkys about representing him."

Badali was then just getting into the business of representing hockey players. The Gretzky family liked his manner. And, when they got to know him, they were convinced he'd be the kind of agent who would be looking out for the best interests of their boy before looking out for himself.

Badali would almost become a member of the family as the relationship grew.

But it could have been Alan Eagleson!

"When we were having all the problems with Wayne's eligibility," remembers McMaster, "we approached Eagleson to be our lawyer. He told us he didn't have time to get involved with kids of that age.

"Wayne really looked up to Alan Eagleson. He liked to refer to him as 'The Eagle'. If he'd been our lawyer I think Wayne would have loved to have been involved with Alan Eagleson."

When Wayne played in the world junior tournament in Montreal against the Russians and kept winning the "Most Valuable Player" award, it was Eagleson who presented it to him.

"I think Eagleson asked him every time he made one of the presentations if Wayne would be his client," McMaster laughed.

Gretzky had his agent by then, of course.

And he was playing for the Sault Ste. Marie Greyhounds, which by that time were being called "Gretzky's Greyhounds."

Gretzky sets to rifle a shot at the net after pulling the netminder out of position
(KEITH STEPHEN, SAULT STE. MARIE STAR)

The Soo Gives Birth to Number 99

He hadn't wanted to go to the Soo at first.
"I hope it's Peterborough," Gretzky told Ted Beare, the *Brantford Expositor* sports editor, before the draft. "They're the best organization in junior A. I might not report if I'm drafted by a northern club like Sudbury or Sault Ste. Marie."

When the Soo drafted him, they were worried he might not report, as had happened to them previously when they drafted Pierre Larouche.

But Gretzky and lawyer Badali headed for Sault Ste. Marie to look the situation over and Gretzky decided to stay.

"It's friendly, more relaxed here," he observed at the time. "It reminds me more of Brantford where I grew up. I played junior B in Toronto for two years but I didn't see much of my team-mates between games."

Gretzky didn't waste any time convincing the doubters as he stepped into junior A hockey at sixteen. In his first exhibition game against Sudbury, Gretzky stole the show. He had a goal and five assists.

Sault Ste. Marie sportswriter, Alex Mitcheli, captured a dressing-room scene after Gretzky scored three goals and three assists to lead the Greyhounds to a 6-1 win over Oshawa Generals in their league opener. Gretzky had received a bottle of Brut as his reward for being named player of the game.

"What's this Brut stuff?" Gretzky asked his team-mates.

"It's after shave lotion," said Greyhound Doug Kimbell.

"After shave lotion," said Wayne. "What am I supposed to do with after shave lotion?"

Two years later, with Gretzky in the National Hockey League, agent Badali would say, "I kid him every day that I wish he'd start shaving so we could get an after shave commercial for him."

Gretzky's coach for the first half of the season in Sault Ste. Marie, until he was replaced by Paul Theriault, was gregarious Muzz MacPherson.

And, oh, the memories he has.

Number 9 was taken

"I'd never seen him play," said MacPherson. "And we picked him third. All I'd heard about him was that he wasn't very big and that there was some question about his skating. A couple of scouts, Fred Litzen and Fred Smith, sat with me one night at the Royal York Hotel in Toronto and said 'relax'.

Wayne poses with Sault Ste. Marie Greyhounds coach Muzz MacPherson
(BOB FROST, SAULT STE. MARIE STAR)

"It didn't take long for me to be impressed with Wayne. The first time I met him was in a hotel room at the Royal York and he was a kid who knew where he was going. Exactly.

"He and his agent, Gus Badali, were hesitant to come to The Soo. They were concerned about ice time. I couldn't guarantee ice time. But I told him we had Craig Hartsburg on the team and the year before was his rookie year with us and he received more than his share of ice time.

"And Wayne had ice time when I was the coach at Sault Ste. Marie. I used him everywhere. I used him on the power play, when we were short-handed, when we were two men short, and the *Sault Ste. Marie Star* was constantly criticizing me for the ice time I gave him. They criticized me because they figured I was burning him out.

"All I know is that when you've got a good hockey player, you use him. I was criticized to death for burning him out. Let me tell you, the guy who is getting the last laugh out of Wayne's career, is me!"

Muzz MacPherson is the man who gave the Great Gretzky the now famous Number 99.

"Brian Gualazzi was on our team the year before and he'd worn number nine," MacPherson remembers. "Wayne wanted number nine. I told Wayne that Brian had the number. If he wanted to give it up, fine, Wayne could have it. But I wasn't going to take it away from him.

"I asked Brian about it, and he said he didn't want to give it up. Not unless he had to.

"So Wayne decided he'd wear number 19.

"I told him that with Phil Esposito and Ken Hodge joining the New York

(BRIAN GAVRILOFF, EDMONTON JOURNAL)

Gretzky with the WHA Oilers

Wayne and Gordie Howe pose for this shot before the game between WHA All-stars and Moscow Dynamo

Line-mates Wayne, Gordie and Mark Howe

Putting pressure on the Dynamo defense

A break in the action to discuss strategy

Wayne listens as the "Master" makes a point

Action between the Edmonton
Oilers and Hartford Whalers

Wayne speeds around a Czech
national defenseman

Number 99 with line-mate B. J. MacDonald

The referee signals a goal as Wayne puts the puck behind Moscow Dynamo goaltender

"Player of the Game," WHA All-stars vs. Moscow Dynamo

A team-mate wisely leaps to let
Wayne get his slapshot away

Total concentration — even on the bench

Rangers and deciding to take numbers 77 and 88 respectively, maybe he ought to consider going up by 11 more and taking 99.

"Wayne was really worried that people would laugh at him if he wore number 99. But I convinced him to try it. They didn't laugh at him."

"I know they expect another guy like Bobby Orr," Gretzky said, at the time, explaining what fans expected of him. "But this is just my first year of junior A hockey. I'm still young. I don't control a game like Craig Hartsburg, but when I get to his age, when I'm eighteen, maybe I'll be good enough to control it."

"It was more hectic when I was ten"

The press attention, in Wayne's year at The Soo, was even greater than it was the year he scored 378 goals in the season he started as a ten-year-old and ended as an eleven-year-old.

Sports Illustrated was following him, the *New York Times* was following him, and he'd spend as long as an hour and a half in the dressing room talking to reporters after games and had to take cabs to get back to the hotel.

But by this time Wayne was an old pro with the media.

One day, he even started to fight back. When *The Weekend Magazine* put in a request to interview the sixteen-year-old, Gretzky agreed but only if it was at 9:30 A.M. and the writer would buy him breakfast. It was the only way he figured he'd get a meal that day. Following the interview he had to meet with a reporter from the *Toronto Sun* and then a reporter from the *Toronto Star* and then he had to show up for film features for television station CBLT and Hockey Night in Canada.

"Really it's not all that bad," Gretzky said that day. "It was more hectic when I was ten."

"At first," recalls MacPherson, "the other players' noses were out of joint. I'd be lying if I said they weren't. But they got used to it. And after a while, watching him be interviewed endlessly, I think there were times they were glad they weren't in his shoes.

"The thing that stopped them from resenting Wayne, though, was that they saw that none of it went to his head.

"The only time he did the 'I'm Wayne Gretzky' routine was funny as hell.

"It was our rookie initiation.

"The year before, in Hartsburg's rookie year, the players made the rookies streak down Queen Street with absolutely nothing on, except for a hockey sock over their heads so nobody would recognize them. I got to meet the mayor of Sault Ste. Marie over that one.

"The next year I decided I'd better get involved in the rookie initiation. Without the rookies' knowledge, of course.

"We set up the same thing. Except that we involved the police in this one.

"All the rookies were in one car, eight of them, and they were all in jockey shorts and nothing else. Wayne was one of the rookies. And just as they were to go streaking, the police car pulled up.

"Wayne thought he could get all of them out of a jam so he jumped out of the car. And he said, 'I'm Wayne Gretzky'.

"The policeman looked at him and said, 'No, you're not. You can't be Wayne Gretzky. I know Muzz MacPherson and I know that he doesn't associate with fags. So you can't be Wayne Gretzky'.

"Wayne didn't know what to say. But I think that made him think about saying 'I'm Wayne Gretzky' after that.

"But he was unbelievably modest. And by Christmas all the resentment had disappeared.

"There's a difference between modesty and dedication to the game, though. I remember once we were on the road and Mike Boyd was giving him a rough time about being glued to a Hockey Night in Canada game on television.

Number 99 poses for this shot during his year with the Greyhounds
(MARGARET CAMERON, SAULT STE. MARIE STAR)

34

"Boyd told him he didn't have to study the game so hard because it would be four years before he'd be in the NHL.

"Wayne gave him a pretty good shot. He said Boyd didn't have to watch the game because they don't televise games in the 'I'. The 'I' stands for the International League.

"I knew Wayne wouldn't be in The Soo for four years. No way."

MacPherson said the other thing that helped Wayne fit in was his sense of humor.

"One night we got beat. Really got beat. I was fuming. When we got home at 3:00 A.M. I made the team go out and skate in the arena with their suits and ties on. All I let them change was their shoes for skates. I made them skate in their suits and ties for forty-five minutes. In the dark.

"The next night we won 8-2. And Wayne, noting that coaches tend to follow the same routine during winning streaks, came up to me after the game and said, 'Gee, coach, I hope you're not superstitious!'"

And, of course, you had to have a sense of humor some nights after playing against Gretzky.

Gary Green, who would later become the coach of the Washington Capitals, came up with an ingenious plan one night to slow Gretzky down.

He informed his players that he would reward them with $2.00 for each hit on Gretzky.

"Some guys had visions of making $50.00," said Green, "but little did they know Wayne Gretzky. All I paid out that night was a buck. Paul MacKinnon had half a hit."

The top rookie

Wayne was hot in his rookie year with the Greyhounds. In September,

Gretzky scored seven goals and added eight assists — in only four games — for fifteen points. In October, in eleven games, he scored eleven goals and twenty-one assists for thirty-three more points. In twelve games in November, he scored fourteen goals and added twenty-one assists for a thirty-five point month. In the five games during December, he added four more goals, nine more assists and thirteen more points. With sixteen goals and twenty-two assists for thirty-eight points, he had his best month in the thirteen games of January.

He came up with his 100th point on January 3rd. His 50th goal on January 28th in Kitchener. His 100th assist on March 10th. In one game, against Windsor, he'd put together seven assists.

And, with a little fatherly advice, he broke the goal scoring record by a rookie.

"My dad told me not to worry about it. He told me the element of surprise could now work for me," Wayne laughed in the post-game dressing room.

Gretzky's parents were among the 4,017 spectators at the Memorial Gardens to watch their son score twice and add two assists in an 11-1 trouncing of Kingston which snapped a four-game goal scoring drought and enabled Wayne to tie the record for goals by a rookie at sixty-seven. He would end up with seventy goals, 112 assists and 182 points to finish second to Ottawa's Bobby Smith.

Gretzky won the Emms Family Trophy for being the league's top rookie and the Bill Hanley Trophy for being the league's most gentlemanly player.

At the end of the season the question was being raised: Had Sault Ste. Marie seen the last of Wayne Gretzky in a Greyhounds' uniform?

Wayne had discussed the possibility of going elsewhere in January at the World Junior Tournament in Montreal.

"At the moment," he was widely quoted as saying, "I would consider it very unlikely that I will play four more years of junior hockey before turning pro. I think I need one more year of junior hockey, a year to grow physically and learn a little more hockey. But by then, I would have a reputation and I think I would be a sitting duck for other players to make a reputation at my expense. I don't want that to happen. There's just too much chance an injury could finish me off before I ever get a chance at the pros. I could go over to Sweden for a couple of years. The risk of injury wouldn't be so great and it would be a good learning experience for my hockey skills. I could play over there for two years and then come back to the NHL when I was eligible."

There were reports that Wayne was unhappy about the amount of school he'd missed.

But it was more than that.

"Wayne is upset with his ice time," said general manager Angelo Bumbacco making reference to the fact that when Theriault took over as coach on February 21st when MacPherson was fired, one of his first priorities was to reduce Gretzky's ice time by as much as ten minutes per game.

MacPherson contends that "Wayne almost went home when they let me go as coach" and he says Wayne Gretzky was the guy who got him the new job as coach of the New Westminster Bruins, owned by Nelson Skalbania, the man who was soon to sign Gretzky to a pro contract.

"I'm convinced I'm in New Westminster because of Wayne Gretzky."

He also figures Wayne would have stayed in The Soo one more year if he were still the coach.

"There's no question about that," MacPherson says. "His dad once told me if I'd stayed, Wayne would have stayed there for another season."

MacPherson's favorite on-ice memory of Gretzky was on Team Canada in the World Junior Tournament in Montreal that year.

"I've seen him score a lot of beautiful goals but he scored one, making a move on a Soviet defenceman, that I can't even describe," he said.

Gretzky impressed more than a few people in that tournament.

He made a believer out of Team Canada co-coach Orval Tessier for one.

"I was skeptical about Gretzky, not having seen him play except once in his own league," said Tessier at the time. "But he's certainly convinced me and everyone else now. He's very intelligent. He has a tremendous amount of puck sense. He's a pleasant surprise."

Gus Bodnar, a former Oshawa Generals coach, took his turn behind the bench and needed no convincing.

"Gretzky's always played two years above his class," said Bodnar at the tournament. "He's just amazing."

Gretzky with line-mates Dan Lucas and Paul Mancini
(KEITH STEPHEN, SAULT STE. MARIE STAR)

4

The Kid Who Entered the World Home for the Aged

When it happened, when Wayne Gretzky signed with the World Hockey Association, it was swift and sudden. It certainly didn't come with the sort of publicity buildup there was over Bobby Hull jumping from the NHL to the WHA. It came with almost no press speculation. The timing of Gretzky's signing was impeccable.

When Nelson Skalbania parked his private jet at Edmonton Industrial Airport at 4:00 P.M. on Sunday, July 11, 1978, and introduced Wayne Gretzky, signed, sealed and delivered for his Indianapolis Racers World Hockey Association franchise, it was perfect.

Twenty-four hours earlier an eighteen-year-old jockey by the name of Steve Cauthen had won his first triple-crown. And twenty-four hours later the NHL annual meetings would begin in Montreal. Skalbania wasn't at all subtle about it. He stopped the plane in Edmonton to announce the story because he wanted the news to get out right then and there. He wanted the NHL owners to swallow their cigars at the meetings.

If there was any inclination to start screaming about the age of the kid Skalbania had just signed up, one had only to think of Cauthen. If there was a Major Junior Jockey League, where would Steve Cauthen be? Riding for $75 a week in Sault Ste. Marie, Kentucky? Besides, Bobby Orr had been an underaged junior. Gordie Howe had been an underaged junior. Why not Wayne Gretzky?

At the time, WHA merger hopes had just been scuttled again. And the signing of Gretzky. . . Well, all's fair in love and war—and the war had just been declared again. Even on day one of Gretzky's pro career, the smart money was saying he was going to be the WHA's hole card for merger.

The teenager from Brantford, the most touted young hockey player and the most eagerly anticipated genius of the national game since Orr, was suddenly a millionaire at seventeen.

A seven-year contract and a dream come true

And there he sat, in the crowded private jet of Vancouver-based entrepreneur Skalbania, fingering a cheque for $50,000—a mere down payment on a seven-year personal services contract estimated to be worth $1.75 million.

"I guess the master plan worked," said Gretzky on the plane as he talked to the *Edmonton Journal's* Jim Matheson in an exclusive interview. "The dream's come true."

Gretzky had contracted to work for Skalbania wherever the owner might go. "Who knows," laughed Skalbania, "he might end up as a deckhand on my boat in the Mediterranean."

The signing, which was completed on a flight from Vancouver to Edmonton with Gretzky's agent, Gus Badali, and Walter and Phyllis Gretzky, was precipitated by Skalbania's dislike for the owners in the National Hockey League. There was no doubt about that. It was rather ironic that two years later, Skalbania, who once owned the WHA Oilers before selling half the team (and finally all the team) to Peter Pocklington, would be one of them as a result of his purchase of the Atlanta Flames and the relocation of the franchise to Calgary. But that was to be another movie.

"I don't really know if this will kill any talk of merger between the two leagues or not," said Skalbania. "But I do know that I didn't like going on my hands and knees begging to get into the NHL last year. Who knows, maybe they'll call a truce now and say enough is enough. The situation, now, is just ridiculous."

Gretzky, six months later, was still marvelling at how he got that first contract from Skalbania, and how crazy it was in the plane, as the deal was struck on that flight from Vancouver to Edmonton in the summer of 1978.

"I had to write it," said The Kid. "I was handed a crumpled sheet of paper. Gus was talking, my dad was too nervous and Skalbania said he couldn't write it because he said the figure made him dizzy."

But the whole thing wasn't a spur of the moment affair on Skalbania's part. Not a bit. Didn't he call a couple of Edmonton media men the night before to ask them if they thought it was a good idea? And he certainly didn't sign the youngster without having watched him perspire.

Skalbania is a noted jogger. He decided he wasn't going to sign an athlete for $1.75 million without at least checking him out to see if he was sound. Skalbania asked Gretzky if he'd like to go for a run. It turned out to be a six-and-a-half-mile marathon.

"It wouldn't have been too bad," said Gretzky. "But it was uphill most of the way."

Gretzky, once a notable Ontario high school runner in the 800 and

1,500 metres, as well as a cross-country competitor, passed with flying colors. Even at this stage of his career, it couldn't be said that he took the money and ran. Skalbania saw to it that he ran before he took the money.

And the money wasn't easy to get used to.

"I still find it hard to believe," Walter Gretzky was saying six months later. "I've worked twenty-two years for Bell Canada and I've never been able to save much money. Now, at seventeen, look how much Wayne has."

But now it was Indianapolis's turn to get to know Gretzky. After the brief stop in Edmonton, the plane continued to Indianapolis where a press conference was to be held the next day.

The signing shook all of hockey

Wayne Fuson, sports editor of the *Indianapolis News* wrote, "The impact of the signing will be to Canadian hockey what Charlie O. Finley's attempted sale of Vida Blue to the Cincinnati Reds was to American League baseball."

A few weeks later, in an interview with *Indianapolis News* hockey writer Dick Denny, Gretzky admitted he felt that impact.

"I knew I would get criticized when I signed with the Racers. When I made my decision to leave junior hockey, I knew I had to stick with it. I don't have any regrets," he told Denny. "All in all, though, I guess my decision really shook Canada. I guess you'd say I'm pretty well known but not as much down here. I was ready for the criticism. I knew it would hit hard. But not that hard. They said I should have waited until I turned twenty."

Gretzky, who took the Indianapolis media men by surprise with the way he handled questions ("I've been interviewed all the time ever since I was six," he had to explain), was introspective enough.

"There will be quite a difference when I start the season, won't there?" said Wayne. "Men! I'll be playing against men. But I don't feel any different when I go onto the ice. Away from the rink I'm not any different than any other teenager."

Back in Canada the media wasn't so concerned with a minor thing like that. There was outrage from the media men who had the NHL logo tattooed on their behinds.

Wayne during a light skate
with the Indianapolis Racers
(BOB DOEPPERS, THE INDIANAPOLIS NEWS)

"A lot of people have said I was foolish not to be thinking of playing sometime in the Stanley Cup play-offs," Gretzky would answer. "But right now the NHL is just going on prestige. It's good. But who is to say it's better than the WHA? I think the WHA has proved to be of equal calibre to the NHL."

Gretzky, after the Indianapolis press conference, would return home to take power-skating lessons. People were still saying he couldn't skate.

"Everything taught in power-skating lessons is designed to help you at some time or another," Gretzky would later explain. "All the Europeans are taught to skate the same way. In Canada everybody learns differently. Power skating helps your strength, balance, and agility and I figured it would improve my acceleration—or starting from a standing position—which was the weakest point of my skating."

When the season started all eyes, as always, would be on Gretzky. Except, of course, Gretzky's. He remembers noticing Robbie Ftorek, the 5'8", 155-pound star of the Cincinnati Stingers.

"After seeing Ftorek, I couldn't help but wonder why everybody was cutting me up about my size," said The Kid, who was then 5'11" and 164 pounds.

Gretzky "only" managed three goals and three assists in his eight games in Indianapolis.

He had two big nights, though.

In one game he scored a goal and added two assists against the Birmingham Bulls. But those statistics were secondary to the bottom-line statistic. The million-dollar baby played that night before a crowd of 1,919 fans in Indianapolis.

Dave Overpeck of the *Indianapolis Star* lectured the fans after that one: "If you are a sports fan at all," he wrote, "you owe it to yourself to come out and watch Wayne Gretzky play hockey. A generation or so from now, you'll be able to tell your grandkids, 'I saw him when he broke into the majors as a seventeen-year-old kid'."

When the Edmonton Oilers came to town, Gretzky scored two goals.

It was interesting, at that moment, to view Gretzky. The first look, of course, was to see if there were any signs of money spoiling the kid. But no matter how hard you looked, it just wasn't there. He may have been worth almost $2 million, but he was still wearing faded blue jeans and sneakers. He was still going to night school twice a week. Still in a room-and-board situation and still living on an allowance of $100 a week. If his Racer team-mates didn't jokingly call him "Brinks," you'd never know he was a millionaire.

"I'm trying to live like any normal seventeen-year-old kid," he said. "I'm living with a family just like I did in junior for two years. I'm enjoying where I'm living. Next year, maybe, I'll live on my own, but now . . ."

Gretzky was living with Dr. Terry Fredericks and his family. And he was still going to grade twelve, attending classes at Broad Ripple High School where he was taking economics and American history.

"The students don't know that much about who I am right now and I'm trying to keep it down as much as possible," he said. "I want to be treated just like anybody else."

That wasn't much of a problem at the Frederick's residence on Windsor Drive in Carmel, Indiana. "I don't think anybody on the block really knew who he was," said Dr. Terry Fredericks. "It was kind of like he was an exchange student. In our area, people didn't follow hockey that much."

One neighbor knew who he was—Don LeRose, the general manager of the Racers. Fredericks happened to be at his house when LeRose had to find a place for Wayne to board.

"We didn't have a teenager in the family," said Sherry Fredericks. "He was just super with our youngsters, Jeff, Brett and Amy. He just fit right in with the family. It was a joy. And not because he was a young superstar. Because he was such a nice young person."

"But the grocery bill was considerably higher than we expected," said Dr. Fredericks. "We couldn't keep him filled up."

Mature beyond his years

The only luxury Gretzky had permitted himself was a Trans-Am car. And even that surprised people. Why not, for example, a Corvette?

"Gus has me on a weekly allowance," said Wayne at the time. "It's not more than any seventeen-year-old would get." Well, maybe a little more?

And, oh yes, there was no girlfriend.

"I'm only seventeen," said Wayne. "And because I've been in four different cities in the last four years I don't have time for a special girl. I have always been taught by my parents to determine my priorities and make sure that they are set. Then you can always have the social life on the side. The girls will always be there."

Now that was maturity!

"The sudden wealth hasn't gone to Wayne's head," said coach Pat Stapleton. "He's had the notoriety for a longer period of time than most kids because of his exploits as a youngster. Wayne came from a humble background. His parents did a good job bringing him up."

"He's mature beyond his years," said Racer team-mate Dave Inkpen.

And on the ice . . .

"Big league hockey is a lot like I expected," Gretzky reported. "Of course, the players are a lot older than in the junior league and a lot more mature. They think a lot faster. They skate a lot faster. And they are a lot stronger. A guy my size and my age has to go out there and outthink them and outsmart them. I've got to use brains instead of brawn."

"He's not going to be a star overnight."

Despite the fact Indianapolis wasn't exactly filling the rink to watch him play—something of a first in Gretzky's career—and that he wasn't exactly leading the scoring race at the time, he was still something to see.

"You keep waiting to see him take his next shift," said WHA executive director Ron Ryan, after his first glimpses of The Boy Wonder. "You sit there and you can't wait for his next shift."

People were still saying he couldn't skate and they were still saying his shot was nothing special and that he certainly didn't have the aggressive qualities of, say, a Bobby Clarke. "But," protested Inkpen, "he sucks you in when you think you've got him cornered."

"He passes the puck better than anybody in hockey," said veteran netminder Gary Smith.

"He has an extra sense," said Stapleton. "And he challenges

defencemen. He has the ability to avoid traffic. He's so deceptive. A pure goal scorer would have a field-day playing with him."

Stapleton admitted he was a little bit leery of The Kid competing with grown men and, as a result, wasn't pushing Gretzky. "I didn't want to get him run down physically or mentally. I knew he'd been compared to Bobby Orr coming out of junior. But there's only one Bobby Orr. Wayne has a great hockey sense, but you've got to have patience. He's not going to be a star overnight."

Oh well. . . Even the people who believed in Gretzky occasionally underestimated his magic.

But there was nothing to misjudge in his character. What you saw was what you got.

"All summer long people kept asking me if I'd met Wayne Gretzky yet," said Indianapolis netminder Eddie Mio back then. "They knew I'd be playing with him and there'd been so much hoopla about his signing for so much money. It was all I heard. Gretzky! Gretzky! Gretzky! Well, then I met him. And talked with him. And I liked him! I realized, as did everybody else, I guess, that all the talk was not his fault. He's sure got the talent and I guess he was paid more for his potential at this point. He's a real personable and likeable kid."

Mio was going to spend more time around Gretzky. But not in Indianapolis.

Wayne ties the goal scoring record for a rookie in OHA Junior A play with goal number 67
(KEITH STEPHEN, SAULT STE. MARIE STAR)

Welcome to pro hockey, kid

In a classic case of *deja vu*, The Kid made it back to the same Edmonton Industrial Airport where Skalbania had landed back in June to announce Gretzky's signing in the first place. Skalbania had decided that the only way to keep the Racers afloat was to unload Gretzky. So it was, "Welcome to pro hockey, kid. You'll be lacing your skates in Edmonton."

He came into Peter Pocklington's possession with Mio and forward Peter Driscoll, and the three flew to Edmonton on a chartered Lear Jet which cost the Oiler owner $7,900. Pocklington has not, to date, complained about the price. It would have been less than that, except that the pilot wanted another $2,500 to fly from the International Airport to the

Industrial Airport. Since they were more than two hours late for a press conference in the Edmonton Inn, Mio signed coach Glen Sather's name to the bill for the extra leg of the flight and they landed a block from the hotel at the Industrial.

"Maybe Nelson should have left me here in June," said Gretzky, who admitted he was a little shocked at the news that he had been sold to the Oilers by Skalbania.

But it could have been the Jets in Winnipeg. And if Jets' owner Michael Gobuty had it to do over again...

"Crazy Nelson," said Gobuty of Skalbania. "Nelson wanted to play backgammon for Gretzky against one-third ownership of the Jets. It was the day before Nelson sold him to Edmonton.

"To my chagrin, I didn't agree to the backgammon game. I found out later that I could have beat him. Nelson, I discovered, really isn't that good a backgammon player."

From that day on, Gobuty would be a permanent fixture on Pocklington's Christmas card list.

"You know, I almost had him without knowing it back in the summer," said Pocklington. "Gretzky's lawyers in Toronto at the time happened to be my lawyers. I told them I'd love to bring this kid to Edmonton. They told me he was too young.

"But a few months later Birmingham Bulls' owner, John Bassett, was talking to Badali about him. The price was too high for Bassett but he told them to get hold of either Pocklington or Skalbania. He'd just been on the phone talking to Skalbania so he suggested Badali should phone him. If he'd been on the phone talking to me..."

When Pocklington's turn did come, the deal for Gretzky wasn't complicated.

"When Nelson sold the Oilers to me, the deal was I'd have to pay him a half million if the Oilers got into the NHL," he said. "I gave him $300,000 cash and we ripped up the agreement for the half million. It was that simple. That's my philosophy. Keep 'em simple. And keep 'em big.

"The whole thing took about five minutes on the phone to finish off. Nelson needed the money right away."

An interesting sidelight to the deal was that the player Indianapolis chose to replace Gretzky was another seventeen-year-old from the Edmonton satellite city of St. Albert. The kid's name was Mark Messier. He was eventually to become an Oiler and Gretzky's team-mate. Messier is only eight days older than Gretzky.

"I was looking for something like this to happen," said Gretzky, who would say nothing negative about Indianapolis.

"In Nelson's eyes, I think he feels he's doing me a favor. He said Edmonton was the best sports city in North America...so I guess we'll see. It's funny though. Here I am, only seventeen, with a three-year head start on most guys, and I've already been traded."

Gretzky wasn't sure about Edmonton right off. "It's a big change, but I'm going to try to meet some kids here. Hopefully, I'm going to go to night school in January, so I'll get to know people there. And I'm pretty sure there's a girl I knew in Sault Ste. Marie who's moved out here..."

Of Gramps and The Kid and the End of the War

ne of the first truly memorable "Gretzky Nights" in pro hockey was December 13, 1978, in Cincinnati, Ohio. And it will probably be unique forever in Gretzky's pro career.

It was the night Wayne Gretzky was benched!

In his game story from Cincinnati, *Edmonton Journal* hockey writer Matheson wrote: "If he'd been in a classroom, Wayne Gretzky probably would have been ordered to write 'I Will Not Be Too Offensive' 500 times on a blackboard. He might even have got a detention."

But since the grade twelve student was playing hockey for a living now, Edmonton Oiler coach Glen Sather resorted to benching the Boy Wonder for the first period of the Oiler-Cincinnati game. Basically for "not helping out enough on defence."

Gretzky responded to the slap on the wrist by coming off the bench to score his first pro hat trick in the final forty minutes.

"He could have sulked," said Sather, who was slightly miffed at the kid's minus-six rating in the first four road-game losses of the trip. "But Wayne got mad instead...the smoke was coming out of his ears."

"I think that game made Wayne Gretzky a hockey player," Sather said later. "That night he stuck it to me, and he carried us to the win."

For sure the soon-to-be-eighteen Gretzky was phenomenal in the final forty minutes of that game. He scored his thirteenth and fourteenth pro goals on plays from behind the net and finished off the three-goal game with a shotgun blast from forty feet out in the third.

Being benched had happened once to Gretzky in junior hockey. "It happened in my last year at Sault Ste. Marie," said Wayne. "I can't remember who we were playing, but I think I got seven points, four of them goals, in the last two periods."

Leduc No. 1 had nothing on Gretzky

By the end of December, they weren't calling him "Brinks" anymore. He was being called The Great Gretzky in Edmonton and while doubts existed throughout the hockey world, especially in NHL circles, Edmonton was convinced.

He'd only been an Edmonton Oiler for one month and twenty-six days. A mere blink of an eye, perhaps. But it was one percent of his life.

And there was no denying The Kid. He was the most exciting thing to happen to Edmonton since oil was discovered at Leduc No. 1 and Jackie Parker led the Eskimos to three straight Canadian Football League championships in the mid-'50s. Every hockey fan in town was convinced he was watching "A Star Is Born." He took fairly ordinary hockey games and turned them into experiences. He took the puck and did things with it that defied the fan to remain unmoved. For six seasons in the WHA the Oilers hadn't really been worth paying to see. But for the last month

and twenty-six days, Wayne Gretzky alone was worth the price of admission and then some. On December twenty-eighth he was only one point out of the WHA's "top 10" in scoring and that was already being recognized as a miracle. Especially considering the weights Sather had tied to his wings.

But he continued to soar. And so did his point totals.

Goaltender Dave Dryden spoke volumes on the subject of Gretzky after a game one night. "Personality-wise, he's incredibly mature. He's thoughtful. He's not the least bit spoiled. And the thing I like best is that he's not self-satisfied. He stays out late after practice. He wants to be as good as he possibly can be. And he's not a follower. He's a leader.

"Talent-wise, his biggest asset is his ability to control the puck and himself. He has the rare ability to wait for somebody to make a little mistake and take advantage of it for everything it's worth. Most players have preconceived notions of what they're going to do. I'm convinced he doesn't."

By now every hockey man in the WHA and dozens of others had compared him to some hockey great or other.

But Dryden recognized his genius back then. "Really, you can't compare him to anybody. He's unique.

"With his talent and with the personality he has shown us so far, the sky is the limit. I've seen a lot of guys with talent who didn't put it to use. But I'm convinced this is one kid who has all sorts of talent and is going to use it all."

That talent has meant that Gretzky's life is one of what most people would describe as daily thrills. But a bigger thrill than he'd ever dreamed of was just around the corner. Wayne Gretzky was to start out the New Year in the kind of situation that would make a public relations man drool.

Howe about that

The Kid, who wouldn't turn eighteen for three more weeks, was to centre a line of Gordie Howe, who had turned fifty and had become a grandfather the year before, and Gordie's twenty-three-year-old son Mark, in the opener of a three-game series between the WHA All-Stars and Moscow Dynamo at the Edmonton Coliseum. The youngest pro hockey player on the same line with the oldest. Number 9 and Number 99.

"I'll be on such a cloud for my first shift with Gordie, it'll be unreal," said Gretzky, who had been treated to what he claimed was the greatest day of his life when he met Gordie Howe in New York the previous summer. Howe had introduced him to singer Debby Boone, boxing great Muhammad Ali, and hockey's Bobby Hull, in that order.

I'll be in a dream when they drop the puck," Gretzky grinned. "I was happy just to be picked to play on the same team with Gordie, but on the same line! Me centering Gordie Howe! I think I might pass him the puck."

When Father Time led The Kid out of the dressing room for that first game of 1979, you just knew the Old Man would have something to say. "Gee, Wayne," the fifty-year-old said to the seventeen-year-old, "I'm nervous."

Howe waited a moment for the reaction.

"He looked at me like I was crazy," giggled Gramps.

Howe, who had played in more all-star games than The Kid had played league games in his pro hockey career, began to laugh.

Moscow Dynamo failed to see the humor in the situation. Thirty-five seconds after the opening face-off, Gretzky scored his first goal.

To Gordie, this playing with a seventeen-year-old who looked like he was going to be a star, wasn't exactly a first.

There was this kid Mark Howe a few years back. But Howe was only forty-five back then. And Wayne Gretzky was only twelve.

While it took a little local press pressure to convince the WHA mental giants the Howe-Gretzky-Howe line was a natural, to say it was a success would qualify as "Understatement of the Year" material. The fans were so captivated by the line, they cheered everytime the trio skated on to the ice. It was a scrumptious scene.

Gretzky tries to be cool as "The Fonz" most times, but this was not a night for cool. The Kid, who already had enough thrills to last a lifetime, was asked to rate it.

"Tops," he said, sounding like a young kid who had just played on the same line as his idol, the greatest player in the history of the game, and scored two goals and added an assist against the Russians to be named "Player of the Game."

Even Old Number Nine was turned on by the situation. He played one of his best games of the season. Gramps was feeling young again. Frisky, even. "This is what keeps me going," said Howe. "It's fun!"

Then he complained that there was no beer in the dressing room. Such was the price of playing with a centre who wasn't old enough to have a beer.

"What's it like playing with your son

and Gretzky?" he was asked.

"We were still the oldest line on the ice," chuckled Howe.

Howe delighted in retelling the stories about all the times he had met Gretzky. "I sort of took him under my wing in New York at the meetings this year," said Howe. "We had a super day. He met Debby Boone and he really got a charge out of that. I told him he must be a *real* rookie, because he didn't even ask her out. We met Muhammad Ali and Bobby Hull and he told me 'I'll never forget this day'.

"He played with my son Murray in Toronto, and I was at a dinner with him once."

"I was ten years old," said Gretzky. "I didn't know what to say, but Gordie helped me out."

"I dropped the puck to him at a bantam tournament once," recalled Gordie.

"I can't remember that," said Gretzky. "But if Mr. Howe said he did, then he did."

Gretzky said he's not sure if he'll believe, even twenty years from now, that as a seventeen-year-old, he played on the same line as fifty-year-old Gordie Howe.

"He's an amazing man," said The Kid.

"He'll never make it," said Howe with a giant grin.

January, 1979, was a month to remember. Not just because of Howe. Gretzky's birthday was coming. And The Kid was growing up a mile a minute.

Left red-faced by a 'movie star'!

The day before he turned eighteen, his team-mates had a little fun with him. For starters, the Oiler players jumped the gun a bit by buying a store-bought cake for him. And then shoved it in his face while a newspaper photographer snapped pictures.

There was one other comedy routine. At practice, Steve Carlson, who had a part in the movie "Slapshot," did his imitation of Gretzky the night before against the New England Whalers.

"It was hilarious," remembers former Oiler public relations director John Short, who caught the act. "They really stuck the needle in pretty good to dramatize Gretzky's act against the Whalers."

What had happened in the game was that Gretzky had been nailed by Gordie Roberts with a bone-jarring check. Gretzky hit the ice and threw his stick and one glove, in a temper tantrum.

"Carlson copied him to the hilt. He almost went so far as to take one of his skates off and throw it."

The red-faced Gretzky watched from the corner.

The Oilers may have been laughing at The Kid and making a point for his benefit (it was his final temper tantrum) in workouts. But they were at a loss for words to describe him in games.

Before his eighteenth birthday Gretzky had exceeded everybody's wildest predictions. He had twenty-three goals and forty-six points in thirty-nine games and was handily leading the Oilers in scoring.

"I remember him telling me he'd be happy with twenty goals and forty assists before the season started," said agent Badali. "The last time I talked to him he thought he might score fifty."

"I'd like to approach Mark Napier's total for an underage player," said Gretzky of another Badali client who fired forty-three goals as a nineteen-

(BRIAN GAVRILOFF, EDMONTON JOURNAL)

(BRIAN GAVRILOFF, EDMONTON JOURNAL)

Wayne signs the contract which will employ him as an Oiler until 1999

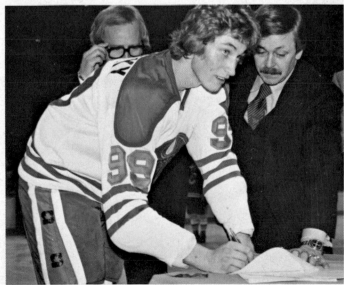

Former GM Larry Gordon and Oiler owner Peter Pocklington look on

Wayne's brothers help him blow
out the candles on the cake
celebrating his eighteenth
birthday and twenty-one-year
contract

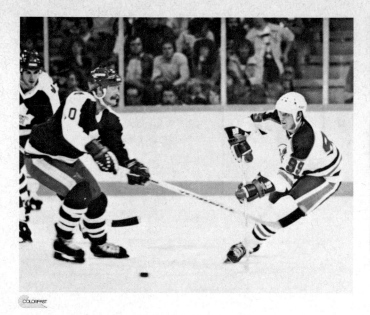

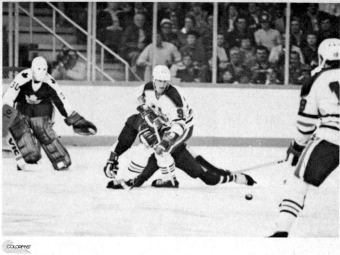

Wayne freewheeling and doing what he does best against the Leafs

On the attack vs.
Vancouver Canucks

Closely watched by Leaf
superstar Borje Salming

A step ahead of a Soviet checker

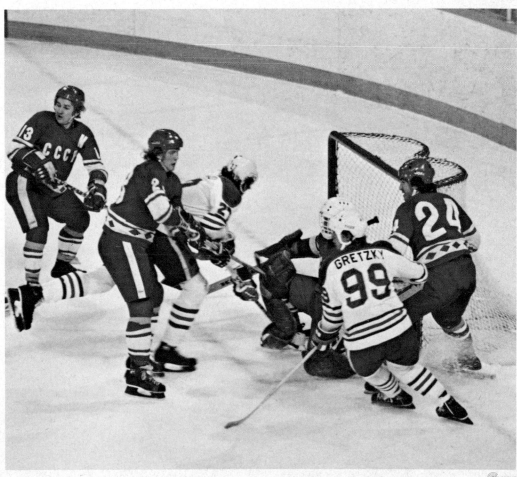

Close-in action between
the Oilers and Soviet
national team

(BRIAN GAVRILOFF, EDMONTON JOURNAL)

year-old with the WHA Toronto Toros in 1975-76.

"On the whole, my biggest adjustment has been realizing that pro goalies are quick learners. You can't beat them with the same moves you used in junior."

Junior. He still had two and a half years of junior eligibility remaining when he said that. And he kept getting reminded of his age.

"I can hardly wait for my birthday," he said often. "I'm tired of reading 'seventeen-year-old Wayne Gretzky' all the time."

One day he went into the lounge at the Edmonton Coliseum after practice with his team-mates. They ordered beer. He had a ginger ale. Gretzky was kicked out. He was too young to be there under Alberta liquor laws. The lounge manager, embarrassed at having to ask the rink's biggest drawing card and the Number One bringer of business to leave, offered to buy Gretzky a drink on his eighteenth birthday. Gretzky said okay, and he even came back and accepted the drink. He took a sip, made one of those faces a kid makes when he's forced to eat his liver, and offered the rest of the drink to someone else at the table.

Scenes like that made it all hard enough to believe. But when you considered that back home in Brantford, Wayne's parents were still collecting family allowance cheques for The Kid...

And what did you get for YOUR birthday?

On January 26, 1978, Wayne Gretzky turned eighteen. And there may never be a birthday quite like it in sport.

You've heard of a 99-year-lease? That's about what Edmonton Oilers had on Number 99 as of 8:09 P.M. on that historic date.

There was a cake in the shape of Number 99. A bottle of sparkling "baby" champagne from his teammates. And the Oilers made it a surprise party for Wayne by flying in his parents, three brothers and his sister.

The birthday party was advertised.

But what came next wasn't.

Pocklington and the Oilers absolutely shocked the 12,321 fans by signing Gretzky, at centre ice, to a twenty-one-year contract. It would keep Gretzky an Oiler until 1999, if all the options were picked up.

How much? It was hard to say. But obviously, it made him a multi-millionaire.

"There's a negotation clause after ten years," said Pocklington. "But there's no out," he quickly added.

"No out," admitted Badali.

"In the tenth year we will sit down and renegotiate because of all the factors such as inflation," said Pocklington. "If we can't agree, an arbitrator will be brought in."

Pocklington swore, that night, that he would not give up Gretzky as a price of merger and Edmonton fans weren't going to let him forget that promise. They wanted into the NHL. But not THAT badly, they didn't.

In many ways, though, as was the case in Skalbania signing Gretzky in the first place, merger was one of the inspirations for the deal.

"We tried to get the rights to the rest of the kids," said Pocklington of the three Gretzky boys, all of whom wore Oiler sweaters with 99 sewn on the back. One of them, eleven-year-old Keith, already had more than 100 goals that season.

"Maybe I'll play with him in six years," said Gretzky, quickly subtracting from seventeen.

That the contract should expire in 1999 wasn't settled until mid-afternoon that day. And according to all, it was more Gretzky's idea than anybody's.

"Gus tried to slow the deal down a little," said the then-Oilers' general manager Larry Gordon. "But Gretzky said he'd seen enough of Edmonton to know this is where he wants to play hockey for the rest of his career."

And there was one other thing. Number 99 liked the ring of 1999.

"Looks like I'm here for life," said Gretzky. "I've played in four different cities in the last three years. I don't need to go move again. Everything is great here. There's no sense to leaving."

For those still looking to see if matters would go to his head, there was little evidence of it. "There's more pressure on me now than ever before," he said in the dressing room after the game that night. "With this contract, I know I'm going to have to go out and earn it."

For the first twenty minutes of the deal it looked as if Pocklington had made a horrendous mistake. Gretzky couldn't have played worse. "I was so uptight I couldn't make a pass," said Wayne. "Heck I could barely write my name on the contract."

More uptight than he was playing on the same line with Gordie Howe in the first game of the WHA All-Star Series with the Soviets?

"I had Gordie Howe to settle me down in that game," The Kid quipped. "I didn't have him tonight."

How good is he, Bobby?

In the weeks that followed everybody in hockey was being sought out for an opinion of Gretzky. Was he going to be the "Next Bobby Orr," as the Oilers were obviously gambling?

In New York, at the NHL Challenge Cup Series with the Soviets, they were even asking Bobby Orr.

"He's good," said Orr. "I watched him in junior and I've heard so much about him that I know he's good. The puck just follows him around."

Orr talked of what it must be like for Gretzky. "I remember the first couple of years. When I was eighteen years old, all I wanted to do was play. I didn't think about anything else. I don't think he's thinking about anything else.

"If he is, consider it advice. You can't get worried reading this and reading that. Enthusiasm is a great thing."

The key, Orr suggested, was having the head to go with the talent. "I'm sure he's so talented he could get by at half speed. But you have to be enthused. You have to play 100 percent all the time. I wanted to play and I loved to play."

Orr was asked how a player in Gretzky's boots should handle the press at that age. Not that it was a problem. Gretzky was doing just fine in that department. But when the question was popped, a couple of veteran NHL reporters, eavesdropping on the conversation, started to laugh. "I never talked to them," he said, motioning at the sportswriters. "I was wrong many times. But I'd sneak away.

"I didn't think about the press clippings," he said. "I wanted to play pro hockey. I'll never forget what a thrill it was when I was told I could check into the Madison Hotel. That was a very exciting day for me. Being told you could check into the Madison Hotel meant you had made the team."

"If he works hard, he'll be very, very successful."

Orr was asked if he had any advice to pass on to The Kid in Edmonton. He took one look at the knee which had ended his career. "First I'd tell him to look after the body."

Bobby Orr said there really wasn't much advice he could give. It's very simple. "Work hard," he said. "He's very, very talented. If he works hard, he'll be very, very successful."

Already in pro company, Gretzky WAS working hard and he WAS becoming very, very successful.

110 points and "Rookie of the Year"

With the Oilers about to play their sixty-second game of the season, he already had eighty points. In his last seventeen games, he had thirty-two points. Almost two points per game. He'd slipped into fifth place in the league scoring race.

"I had some goals when I turned pro," Gretzky was admitting to the press now. "Twenty goals and forty assists."

On April tenth, he scored goals 39, 40, and 41. And got his fifty-eighth assist. That gave him 99 points, and considering his sweater number, it might have been a nice total to end with. But he closed with 110 points, finishing third in the WHA scoring race and winning WHA "Rookie of the Year" honors. The Oilers had finished atop the WHA for the first time ever and they should have won it all. But

they lost out in what was to be the final Avco Cup playoffs. While they reached the final, the Oilers were beaten by the Winnipeg Jets and, in a typically candid comment the following year as Oilers were struggling to make the playoffs, a big part of the Gretzky character shone through.

He'd long since proved he was an eighteen-year-old kid with a twenty-eight-year-old head on his shoulders.

And on this night in Chicago, Gretzky pointed to a naked finger on his right hand. "There should be an Avco Cup ring there," he said. "We had the better team. But we ended up losers. And that's been in the back of my mind ever since. We had the better team but we didn't win. This year we've got the best team of the ones in the race for the last few playoff spots. If we don't make the playoffs, we've wasted the year. If we don't make the playoffs, we'll go to camp in September and we'll more or less be starting from scratch all over again. The whole thing about this year, because we're young and we're in our first year in the NHL, is to gain experience. To develop character as a team. If we don't make the playoffs, we'll go to camp and we'll be starting all over again."

But that was a year ahead of time.

Edmonton and the three other WHA teams had just been accepted into the NHL. And it was another sporting thrill for a city that used to be something of a pimple on the prairie, and was now experiencing what it was like to be big league. Gretzky was a big part of that. But not the only part.

Gretzky attracts a lot of attention wherever he goes
(BRIAN J. GAVRILOFF, EDMONTON JOURNAL)

CHAPTER

Gretzky Tackles the NHL Mystique

The 1978 Commonwealth Games were a tremendous success, the Edmonton Eskimos won the Grey Cup, the Oilers made it into the National Hockey League, and owner Pocklington had purchased the Oakland Stompers of the North American Soccer League to bring to the city under the name of the Edmonton Drillers — things were happening on all fronts. Gretzky's faith in the city, as shown by his willingness to sign a twenty-one-year contract, wasn't without justification.

In the month the Oilers put their season tickets on sale, competition for the sports dollar was fierce. The Eskimos were in the middle of their annual season-ticket drive. The Drillers, who showed up in town a month before they were to play their first game, were also selling season tickets. The Oilers and Eskimos sold out in a flash. And the Drillers did surprisingly well considering the circumstances. In one month, more than $10 million of season-ticket business was done in Edmonton.

But NHL talk was dominating the coffee breaks. And the biggest discussion was how Wayne Gretzky would do under the Big Top. Nor was it restricted to Edmonton coffee shops. There was the same sort of talk in the other twenty NHL cities. "He won't do much next year. The checking is tighter in the NHL. They'll hit him. He'll be lucky to score twenty." That's what they were saying.

Gretzky heard the talk. And he wasn't buying it. "This is my fourth year as a 'rookie'," said the one and only individual player who was a factor in merger.

"Each year I've had to prove myself. Each year they told me the checking would be tighter. Each year they told me I'd get hit more. Each year they told me I wouldn't score. Every year I've been told I'm going to get run out of the rink.

"Next year will be my fifth year as a 'rookie'. I'll be going into the NHL at eighteen, just like Bobby Orr and Gordie Howe. There's going to be a lot of pressure. But I plan to prove myself next year too."

When owner Pocklington heard that he smiled. "It's going to be fun growing up with Gretzky. As he gets older, I'm going to get younger."

With Peter Pocklington acting like a proud papa, and all of Edmonton like a city of 600,000 adopted relatives, there was still the matter of returning to the real hometown—the real family and old friends—in Brantford.

Old friends wondered if he'd still talk to them

What was it like in Brantford after that marvelous first season in pro hockey and with a twenty-one-year contract with the Edmonton Oilers— the *National Hockey League* Edmonton Oilers—in his back pocket?

"It was a little weird," remembered Gretzky, who had returned to Edmonton in September as the same kid he was when he left—except his acne condition was a little better now.

"The phone never stopped ringing. And there were a lot of people who wanted autographs and stuff. But the people I used to know reacted a bit different too. I'd walk down the street and see people I knew and they'd be a bit edgy. I think they wondered if I'd still talk to them or something dumb like that. That's a funny feeling. But it didn't take long for me to convince them I hadn't changed much."

And he hadn't.

There were to be some changes in his lifestyle. But not many.

"I was thinking of going out and looking for an apartment," he said. "But I don't know. A lot of guys my age are still boarding while they play junior hockey. There's nothing wrong with it. I think I'll take my time and see what happens."

To be eighteen and not have to go to rookie camp

While it was "Back to Camp" for most hockey players, it was more than that for Gretzky. It was also "Back to School" like it was for most kids his age.

Ross Sheppard Composite High School.

And he wasn't planning to go incognito. "I don't think I'll be wearing a mask or growing a moustache or anything like that," chuckled Gretzky. It wasn't to be for long. He only had two credits to go to get his high school diploma. With his next twenty-one years covered by contract, Gretzky certainly didn't need school to make a living.

"Why?" seemed like a logical question.

"I promised my parents that I'd complete grade twelve," he said. "I also think going to school will keep my mind thinking. Keep me sharper. And it'll give me something to do on road trips. You can't read *The Hockey News* all day. I need Canadian history and English. My classes are in the afternoon. We practice in the morning. With two classes I should have no problems with road trips."

Meanwhile, the strangest sight at training camp was Gretzky, sitting in the stands, watching rookie camp.

"It's a funny feeling when you're eighteen and you don't have to attend rookie camp," he said. "Everybody there is older than I am."

"Hoo boy — I can't believe this is happening."

In pre-season, Gretzky picked up where he'd left off. And after one look, people like Phil Esposito of the New York Rangers were willing to admit everything they had heard about the kid had to be true. Gretzky scored five points in twenty-one minutes against the Rangers and in the post-game dressing room Esposito said, "He's the greatest young player I've seen since Bobby Orr."

The Oilers played their first National Hockey League game in Chicago. And all eyes, of course, were on Gretzky.

It was two hours before game time and in the bowels of Chicago Stadium, Edmonton Oilers were not only getting themselves up for the game, they were getting up-tight and out of sight.

"Hoo boy," said Wayne Gretzky. "I can't believe this is happening."

Before the game he was featured in both Chicago major daily newspapers and one front sports page interview carried the now usual "Great Gretzky" headline.

"When they play the national anthems, I know I'm going to get but-

terflies," he sighed.

Butterflies, however, are wee things. After the historic first Oiler game in the NHL was over, Gretzky and virtually all the Oilers admitted the things fluttering in their stomachs had a considerably larger wing span.

"I've never been that nervous before a game in my life," The Kid said, even counting the night he had played with Howe in the WHA all-star game and the night he'd signed the twenty-one-year deal.

Mark Messier, Oilers' other eighteen-year-old, said if Gretzky was nervous, he was petrified. "It really hit me in the afternoon," said Messier. "I sat in my hotel room and all I could think about was 'Hey, we're in the NHL.' It got to me."

It got to all the Oilers. They were an early disaster. People back in Edmonton, watching on television, had to be thinking for the first few minutes of the game that it was going to be a long year. Or decade. But the Oilers overcame their nerves to some extent, and nearly came back to win.

Rookie Kevin Lowe scored the first Oiler goal in NHL history with Gretzky drawing an assist. Gretzky was named the third star of the game.

Wayne and Kevin Lowe — the 'Odd Couple'

Lowe also settled Gretzky's quandary over whether to remain on room-and-board or get an apartment. The apartment won.

We take you now to a modest four-storey walk-up on Edmonton's South Side where we look in on Felix Lowe and Oscar Gretzky. "I wouldn't say Gretz is a terrible cook," says Lowe, the captain of the Quebec Remparts the year before, and Oilers' first pick in the NHL draft. "It's just that I'm a better cook than he is.

"And I don't know if I should be saying it," he added, "but Gretz isn't doing too much homework so far. I'm going to have to get on him about that."

The two worked out a deal with a fourteen-year-old girl of the family across the hall. She vacuums the apartment in exchange for hockey tickets.

Gretzky was in awe of Lowe's cooking.

"He's amazing," The Kid said. "Kevin cooks roasts, makes fondues and bakes lasagna. One night he even had a huge cherry cheesecake for dessert."

"I can't be that good," said Lowe. "I can't get him fattened up."

It was a great scene with those two kids the first few weeks. They were still young enough to talk about being thrilled without feeling as if it was unprofessional, or uncool.

"It's twice as much as I thought it would be," said Lowe of the NHL experience. "The excitement and glamor is incredible. In junior hockey I was a pretty popular person. But in pro, it's already way above that. It's more than I thought it would be. A lot more."

Lowe said he was delighted to be living with Gretzky because he felt some of the good things about his roomie were rubbing off on him. "At least, I hope so," he said. "He's unaffected. A lot of guys would have blown the situation Gretz is in. He's younger than I am. But it doesn't feel that way. We're getting on great as roomies. And he really isn't THAT bad a cook.

"We think a lot alike. We're both shooting for the same sort of thing. I know I'm not going to be content just being a fringe Oiler. I want to be a star. Gretz is a star already. But he wants to be the calibre of somebody like Guy Lafleur. I think we're both the kind of guys who are going to work every night to try to be as good as we can possibly become."

They're the Odd Couple all right. Odd in that it was amazing to find a couple of kids with their heads screwed on straight living under the same roof. So many young, suddenly-rich pro hockey players react badly to adulation and money.

By now Wayne Gretzky couldn't find a place in Edmonton where he wouldn't be recognized. But it wasn't turning him into a recluse.

"I still find it kind of neat to walk down the street and have someone know who I am and to want my autograph," he said. "I guess I take a bit of pride in that because it means I've done something people like."

On the subject of autographs...

"I don't mind the autograph hunters because I can remember my mother and one of her friends chasing after Bobby Hull to get his autograph for me when I was seven," he'd said.

But odd as it may have seemed for an eighteen-year-old who had written as much history as Gretzky, Edmonton was already starting to take him a little for granted.

Somehow, it seemed, he'd been thrilling Edmonton fans forever when he stepped on the ice against the New York Islanders on November 2nd. One year ago to the day, Wayne Gretzky had played his first game as an Edmonton Oiler.

A big win for the Oilers and 'first star' for Gretzky

The scene that night might be forever etched in the minds of the 15,418 who were there to watch the Oilers stun the Islanders 7-5. With thirty seconds to go, the fans were standing, hooting, and howling. But the crowd response to remember was when Gretzky was announced as the first star of the game. It wasn't a continuation of the din. It was more a polite, appreciative response. It was as if the crowd was saying "of course."

The Kid put on his greatest show in the NHL to that point. And it wasn't the two goals and an assist. Gretzky watchers were virtually unanimous about it. They'd never seen The Kid play better. And it was his first game back after missing a game and three-quarters because of tonsillitis. If his line-mates had hit the net half the times he set them up, Gretzky would have had half a dozen points, easy.

"Gretzky made me look like a donkey," summarized Islander goaltender Glenn "Chico" Resch.

Oiler coach Sather said Gretzky's first shift in the game said it all about The Kid. "The Islanders scored in the second minute of the game and their goal was Gretzky's fault. His mistake. And he knew it. He looked at me on the bench and I knew by his expression he knew it. He wanted to get out there and get it back right then and there. That's why he shot like he did."

Gretzky came back and scored on the Oilers' first shot on goal twenty-one seconds later. "That's the hardest shot I've ever taken in my life," said Gretzky. But then he showed his Gordie Howe-like ability to downgrade himself. "To be honest, I was shooting for the other side of the net."

Gretzky had four goals and nine assists at this point.

"Things just happen when he's out there," said line-mate Blair Mac-Donald, who wasn't ashamed to admit much of his success was due to Gretzky's playmaking. "It's unbelievable how much he's matured as a playmaker. Last year he'd often just get to the blueline and shoot. But he learns fast. Now he gets to the blueline and waits for his three or four options."

"I'll tell you one thing," said Sather on Gretzky's first anniversary as an Oiler. "I wouldn't trade him for four New York Rangers AND Barry Beck. Oops! You know what I just did? I just compared him to somebody. That's the first time I ever compared Wayne Gretzky to anybody. I promised him when he came here that I wouldn't put any pressure on him by doing that."

But by this point he'd been compared in some way or another to just about every great who ever played the game.

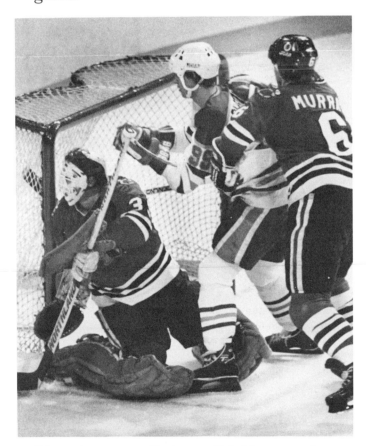

Wayne is squeezed between Bob Murray and Tony 'O' Esposito in a game with the Chicago Black Hawks
(BRIAN J. GAVRILOFF, EDMONTON JOURNAL)

The NHL scoring race — "You mean beat Jesus and God?"

On January 24, in preparing to play a game against the Toronto Maple Leafs on the first anniversary of his signing the twenty-one-year deal at centre ice in the Edmonton Coliseum, Gretzky made what would prove to be an interesting statement.

Asked if he thought he'd win the NHL scoring championship, he looked appalled. "You mean, beat Jesus and God?" he said.

Marcel Dionne and Guy Lafleur, he was willing to concede, were better than he was.

But the rest of the best in the NHL?

"I'm as good as they are," The Kid had decided. "The key is to keep telling myself that I'm as good as they are."

The night before, with nineteen seconds remaining, Gretzky scored his fifth winning goal of the season. It was his first winner at home in the NHL. The other four were on the road. That number was significant in that it was the exact number of wins Oilers had on the road.

Gunning for third but look out above!

With an assist earlier in the game against the Los Angeles Kings, Gretzky had moved into a tie with Charlie Simmer for fourth place in the NHL scoring race. And he was only three points behind third-place Dave Taylor. Edmonton had thirteen wins, and another revealing statistic was that Gretzky had thirty-two points in those wins. With twenty-six goals and forty-three assists, he was ahead of the pace from the year before when he scored forty-six goals and 110 points in the WHA.

You remember that league, the WHA, variously known in NHL circles as the Wishful Hockey Association, the Won't Hit Association, and the World Home for the Aged. A league which was supposed to be so inferior because it had a fifty-one-year-old man playing in it?

Gretzky at this point had 176 points in 125 games as a pro and he still had 112 games to play before he would have used up all his junior hockey eligibility.

Well, maybe, just maybe, all those people who said he'd be nothing special in the NHL were all wrong, hmmm?

"At the start of the season there were a lot of people who were still saying I couldn't play in the NHL," said Gretzky, opening a subject he hadn't dealt with since prior to the season — when he'd calmly predicted he'd prove them wrong, just as he'd done the year before in the WHA.

Gretzky was admitting now that he had set a goal for himself early in the season. He said he'd made up his mind that he wanted to finish third in the NHL scoring race.

He set that goal, he said, about two hours before game time one night in Maple Leaf Gardens after reading a program article about himself.

"It was all about what a good year I had last year in the World Hockey Association and it was really complimentary and everything. It predicted I'd probably do okay in the NHL but the last line of the article said I'd finished third in scoring in the WHA last year, but of course, there was no way I'd finish third in the NHL this year."

Once he drilled it through his head not to be in awe of the other stars,

"Jesus" and "God" excepted, Gretzky figured he was on his way.

"Three years ago I was in the stands watching Gil Perreault and I was thinking he was the greatest. Now I have to go on the same ice with him and convince myself that I am as good as he is," said Gretzky, who admits he's been able to get up more for the games against the top players, when the challenge of proving himself by comparison was right there for all to see. Especially in their rinks. And Gretzky, at this point, had scored more goals on the road than he had at home.

"A lot of players get psyched out by all the talk. Like everybody tried to convince me that I'd really notice a difference in the hitting and checking in the NHL. I thought it would be tougher hockey than it is. I thought it would be more physical.

"A lot of players come into the NHL and get down on themselves. They get psyched out by just being in the NHL, by going on the road and by thinking all these guys are great."

The trophy they wouldn't allow him to win

But all those guys aren't Wayne Gretzkys. And by the All-Star break, Gretzky's accomplishments had reached the point where they'd already passed "remarkable" and "amazing" and had truly reached mind-boggling status.

And there began to stir a cry of "unfair" in Edmonton. A cry to make Wayne Gretzky eligible for the Calder Trophy as "Rookie of the Year" in the NHL. It was already becoming quite clear this young man was the best "first year" player in the NHL. Maybe the greatest "first year" player in history.

There was also quite the contradiction. The NHL wouldn't permit Gretzky "Rookie of the Year" status because he had one year of major league hockey in the WHA. And yet the NHL wouldn't count his WHA totals in the NHL record book because the WHA was a minor league.

Jim Coleman, nationally syndicated sports columnist of the Southam News Service, made the point:

> Up until the current season, the rules for awarding the Calder Trophy, as printed in the NHL's official guidebook, were: 'To the player selected as the most proficient in his first season of competition in the National Hockey League.' The rule also stipulated that 'the player cannot have played more than twenty-five games in any single preceding season, not in six or more games in each of any two preceding seasons.'

> Before the opening of the 1979-80 season, the rule was amended by the addition of the following five words: 'In any major professional league.'

> As most fair-minded sports commentators across the country have been pointing out, the NHL amendment of its own rule appears to be aimed directly at Wayne Gretzky—although he hadn't even played his first NHL game when the change was made. Up until last summer's amalgamation, most of the NHL Big Domes scornfully had declined to admit that the WHA was a major league.

A goal against the New England Whalers signalled by the now-famous patented Gretzky kick
(KEN ORR, EDMONTON JOURNAL)

The Old Records Fall

As he headed for the NHL All-Star Game in Detroit, having just turned nineteen, Gretzky had thirty-two goals and fifty-two assists for eighty-four points. In his last nine games, Gretzky, who had registered his first three-goal game the week before against Winnipeg Jets, had nine goals and thirteen assists for twenty-two points. He was now only fifteen points behind Dionne and ten behind Lafleur. And people were beginning to think the "unthinkable"—that Gretzky could catch "Jesus" and "God."

With twenty-eight games to go, Gretzky had already passed Marcel Dionne's first-year total of seventy-seven points.

Having scored eleven points in his last three games, this Wonderkid had also passed Richard Martin's first-year total of seventy-four. And Bobby Smith's first-year total, also seventy-four.

Gilbert Perreault, in his first year, had seventy-four points. Guy Lafleur had sixty-four. Seven more and Gretzky would tie Mike Bossy's first-year total. And with twelve more he'd become the highest first-year point producer in this history of the game, surpassing Bryan Trottier's ninety-five. There was no doubt he'd smash that record to smithereens. But he wasn't eligible for the Calder.

No argument — a place in history

There was one record, however, they couldn't do anything about. That came on the night of February 15 against the Washington Capitals. Gretzky took up official record residence on page 136 of the NHL record book, as he scored seven assists in one game. His room-mate, record-wise, was Billy Taylor, who had held the old mark since March 16, 1947.

Gretzky, who had one five-point night and two four-pointers earlier in the season, was prepared for the big night. "I just had a feeling I might explode," he said. "Every time I passed the puck, somebody seemed to put it in."

Well, almost every time.

Al Hamilton, the only original Oiler from the first year in the WHA still with the club at the time, missed one late in the game. Gretzky had slipped Hamilton a perfect pass twenty feet in front of Capitals' netminder Wayne Stephenson but Hamilton's shot sailed wide.

"I blew it," said Hamilton. "If I'd scored, he would have been in the record book alone. But that's show biz."

"Tonight we just sat back and watched," whistled team-mate Dave Hunter. "Was this Gretzky's night or what?"

Brantford's "Athlete of the Year"

He'd been the biggest thing in the city of 69,000 since he was four feet tall and seventy-eight pounds in pee wee hockey. But until Friday, March 28, 1979, Wayne Gretzky had never been the "Athlete of the Year" in Brantford.

"Who won it before? Well, Gary Summerhays, the boxer, won it a lot

of times," said Wayne when he was asked for a little background on the subject.

"I guess I've got about 100 awards over the years," added Wayne, who only weeks earlier was an unanimous choice as Edmonton's Athlete of the Year. "But this is a new one. My dad says I can have them all when I get married and have a house of my own. But he's gotta be kidding. They'd take up too much room."

Gretzky, though, wasn't in any way putting down the award or what the occasion meant to him. "It meant a lot," he said. "And it meant just as much and more to my mom and dad. I mean, it's my home town."

The Oilers produced a chauffeur-driven limousine to carry Gretzky, Badali, Sather, and a few team-mates to Brantford for the affair which included a dinner, and a puck-dropping ceremony for an exhibition game between two junior B teams, comprised of many of Gretzky's childhood chums to commemorate the occasion.

The next night Wayne Gretzky would play his greatest game. It was a Hockey Night in Canada game and if there were any doubters left, this one quieted them.

Showcase night in Canada — removing all doubts

Two goals. Six points. He was simply a one-man show against the Toronto Maple Leafs that night. Spectacular! In his last eight games — seven of which the Oilers won to move back into the race for a playoff position — Gretzky had scored ten goals. A couple of nights earlier against Atlanta on the road, Gretzky had scored his forty-sixth and forty-seventh goals and set up the winner with 1:50 to play. Every night he'd contributed. Every night the story was virtually the same. Ron Low, a recent acquisition in goal from the Quebec Nordiques, would hold the Oilers in early and Gretzky would win it late. The two of them were working miracles. Ten goals in eight games for Gretzky down the stretch. And twenty-four points!

And Gretzky was making a run at the scoring title.

In Brantford, the Gretzkys received "a record" thirty phone calls after the Hockey Night in Canada game from Brantford well-wishers. One of those calls came from the Ferris family of Brantford, who had taken a banner which received almost as much exposure as Gretzky during the telecast. The banner featured Marcel Dionne's total and Gretzky's changing total. Gretzky started the night with 127 points, six behind Dionne. He ended up with 133 and tied for the lead in the scoring race. Both the Oilers and the Los Angeles Kings, Gretzky and Dionne, had three games to play.

The night Gretzky had in Maple Leaf Gardens offered another insight into The Kid. Unquestionably the Toronto papers had provided Gretzky with more "ink" on a game day than he'd ever had in his life.

"It puts extra pressure on me," said Gretzky. "When the press is building mc up, it promotes hockey and helps put people in the building. I guess I get out there and try espcially hard to make sure I do as well as the press says I can do. Then, of course, there are the people who are coming to see me flop. And that's the other side of the coin."

With "Wayne Gretzky Day" in Brantford, all the publicity in Toronto, and a rare Oiler game on Hockey Night in Canada's national network, there was no lack of pres-sure. And when it was over, there was no lack of total, unrestrained, unre-served adulation for The Kid. Canada was, finally, sold on him.

The Butler did it

A few days after the Toronto game most of the hockey people who still possessed some sort of theory that Gretzky could be stopped and would be stopped the following year, may have been able to hold out some "hope" for the future.

They were all big games now, for the Oilers as a team, and for Gretzky in the scoring race. The next one was in Vancouver and the Canucks, too, were battling for a playoff berth with three games remaining.

And, when it was over, it could be said "The Butler did it!"

Stop Wayne Gretzky and you stop the Edmonton Oilers. That was the game plan for the Canucks. And it worked. Oh, how it worked!

Molson Breweries had spent $400 to set up a "clinch the playoff spot" party for the Oilers after the game in the Pacific Coliseum, but thanks to the checking job of Canuck winger Jerry Butler, the Canucks humiliated the uptight Oilers 5-0 and moved into a three-way tie with the Washington Capitals and the Oilers for the final two playoff spots.

Gretzky wasn't held off the scoresheet for long. Only two games remained and the Minnesota North Stars, a team which had checked Gretzky with more success than most, were visitors in Edmonton.

Oilers only managed one goal in the game. But it was Gretzky who scored. Dave Hunter sent a forty-five-foot shot at the Minnesota goal and Gretzky rapped the puck into the net with his back to the goal. And it was a 1-1 tie.

71

With Gretzky on the rampage, the Oilers had only the Vancouver loss in their last ten games.

It was number 50 for Gretzky.

Gretzky put on a tremendous show. He had six shots and sent a half-dozen team-mates in on net with excellent opportunities they missed.

The season was summed up perfectly with the *Edmonton Journal* headline after the final game: "OILERS ARE PLAYOFF BOUND," was the overline, "ABOARD THE GRETZKY EXPRESS."

Edmonton beat Colorado 6-1. And Gretzky scored Number 51 and added two assists.

The Kid could hardly talk after the game because of the tonsillitis. He admitted he was weak. And he didn't think he played that well.

Neither did Bobby Schmautz, his former Oiler team-mate who was back with former Bruin coach Don Cherry in Colorado. "Even on the nights when he doesn't play real well," said Schmautz, a former team-mate of Bobby Orr, "he still gets three or four points. The great ones can do that. I can remember Orr getting two goals and two assists on nights when he wasn't on, too."

Being there was everything in the first year

Ah, the playoffs!

Being there, of course, was everything for the Oilers in their first NHL season. "When you've been there, you know how to get there," Gretzky said. "And that's what this whole season was all about to me."

The Oilers were now winners, not losers. So easily could it have been the other way: going to training camp in September, and wondering if they knew how to win.

The Oilers, Gretzky said, would have that playoff experience to draw from for the next year. And they'd be a better team because of it.

"We won't be like Colorado and maybe Washington. They've never been there. We won't have to go through that," explained The Kid.

"This team will be playing in the Stanley Cup finals in three or four years," said Ron Low. "Any team with Wayne Gretzky on it, has to be. He's that good."

When the losers were winners

History would record a Philadelphia Flyers sweep over the Oilers. One. Two. Three. No runs. No hits. No errors. Nobody left on base. A first-place team wiping out a sixteenth-place team in straight games. History unfolding as it should.

But in this case, history would be full of beans.

Twice the Oilers took the Flyers into overtime, once in Philadelphia in the first game of the best-of-five series. And then, the third game, the Oilers took Philadelphia into DOUBLE overtime before losing on a goal by Bobby Clarke.

"They should be damn proud of themselves in that other dressing room," said Flyers' coach Pat Quinn of the team which had to win eight and tie one of their last eleven games to get into the playoffs on the last day of the season. "They showed us their mettle. They showed what they're made of and what they're going to do in the future."

Clarke said it really wasn't fair that the Oilers didn't win a game.

"Let's face it," he said. "The whole series could have gone either way. We could just as easily be down 2-1 today as series winners in three straight

(BRIAN J. GAVRILOFF, EDMONTON JOURNAL)

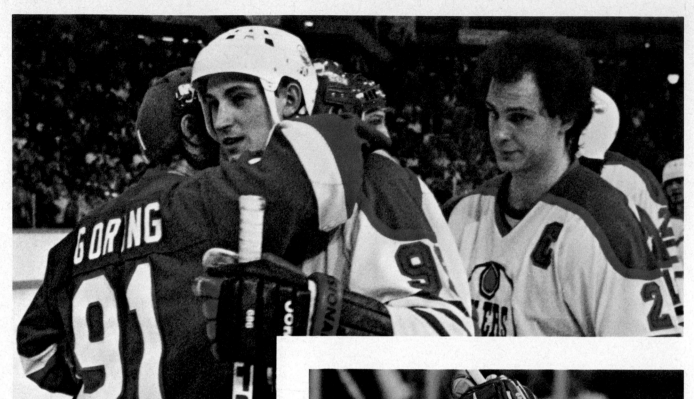

Butch Goring and Wayne embrace after a
hard-fought Stanley Cup '81
semi-final series that went to six games
in favor of the Islanders.

(BRIAN J. GAVRILOFF, EDMONTON JOURNAL)

Wayne signals a goal in the
1981 Canada Cup series.

(BRIAN J. GAVRILOFF, EDMONTON JOURNAL)

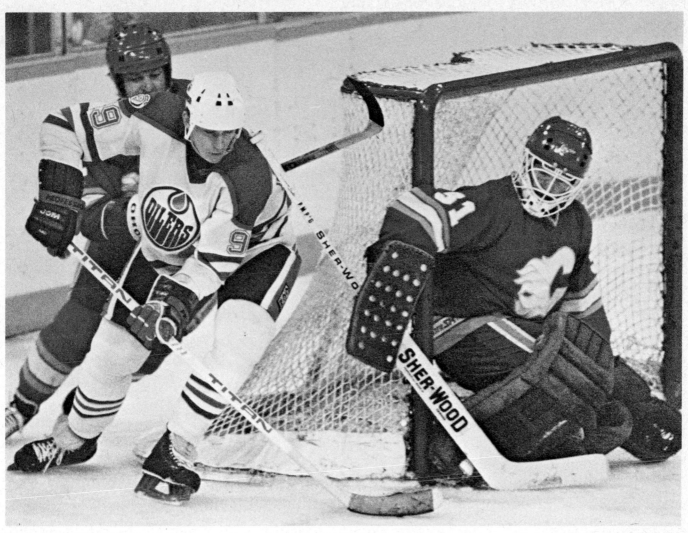

Wayne circles the Calgary net.
(BRIAN J. GAVRILOFF, EDMONTON JOURNAL)

Wayne loves to score even if he has to carry the puck over the goal line himself.
(BRIAN J. GAVRILOFF, EDMONTON JOURNAL)

A happy Wayne Gretzky being interviewed after scoring goals No. 77, 78 and 79 vs. Buffalo to break Phil Esposito's single-season goal-scoring record of 76.
(BRIAN J. GAVRILOFF, EDMONTON JOURNAL)

Pocklington hugs his investment in the locker room after the Buffalo game.
(BRIAN J. GAVRILOFF, EDMONTON JOURNAL)

Digging hard vs. the North Stars.
(BRIAN J. GAVRILOFF, EDMONTON JOURNAL)

Wayne in action vs. Hartford Whalers.
(BRIAN J. GAVRILOFF, EDMONTON JOURNAL)

Two superstars—Wayne and Rod Stewart.
(BRIAN J. GAVRILOFF, EDMONTON JOURNAL)

Theresa Heise—Wayne's fan for life.
(BRIAN J. GAVRILOFF, EDMONTON JOURNAL)

Theresa Heise of Edmonton gets her "dream of a lifetime."
(BRIAN J. GAVRILOFF, EDMONTON JOURNAL)

Gretzky scores goal no. 76 in Detroit. Team-mates Lumley, Fogalin and Lowe offer congratulations. (top photo)

The Oilers go crazy after Wayne scores No. 77.

(BRIAN J. GAVRILOFF, EDMONTON JOURNAL)

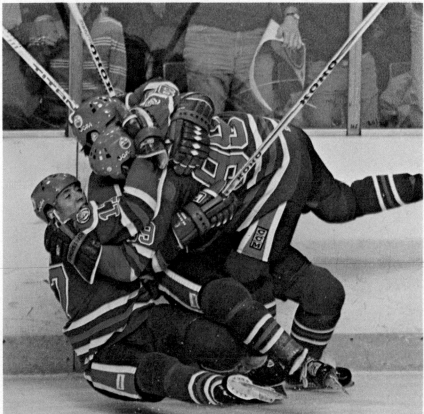

Signing autographs is one thing that Wayne never seems to tire of. Here he's standing outside the Oilers' dressing room.

games. There's no way they'll be a sixteenth-place team next year. Not with this experience. Not with Low playing like that for them in goal. And certainly not with Wayne Gretzky and Mark Messier. They're both, obviously, outstanding. The only thing that beat them in this series was our experience."

"Now they've got the experience of a playoff drive and a playoff series," said Bill Barber. "And of course, they've got Gretzky."

The King is retired; 'Long Live the King'

"BYNG-O!" screamed the *Edmonton Journal* front page headline on June 5, "THE KID HAS HART."

It was a day like no other in hockey history. On the same day Number 9 officially retired from hockey, Number 99, The Great Gretzky officially ascended his throne.

It was only two years earlier that Howe met Gretzky at a World Hockey Association function in New York and now Wayne was telling the world that Gordie had given him some advice he planned to live up to for his entire career.

"Gordie just told me to give it everything I had every day to try to earn my money and to try to blot out the rest. If I did that, he said, when I left the game, I'd be able to leave it without any regrets."

Howe left the game without any regrets that day and Gretzky reaped his first rewards.

Wayne goes for a tumble.

(BRIAN J. GAVRILOFF, EDMONTON JOURNAL)

He was informed that day, by Peter Pocklington, that he'd won both the Hart Trophy as the Most Valuable Player in the League and the Lady Byng Trophy as the player best combining ability and sportsmanship. At nineteen, he was the youngest player to win either award. And only four times in the entire history of the NHL had one player been so honored with both awards in the same year, the most recent being Stan Mikita in 1968.

"I remember when I was in Montreal at the award ceremonies last year and I saw those trophies. There were a lot of people kidding me when I looked at them. But I made up my mind when I looked at the Hart, that someday I'd have my name on that one. I felt then, if I tried as hard as I could, I'd be able to do it. I've always thought that there's no use shooting for a medium goal. You have to shoot for the highest goal. And other than the Stanley Cup, that's the greatest trophy there is in the NHL."

But the really mind-boggling aspect of it all wasn't just somebody his age winning the Hart and the Lady Byng. It was the fact he should have also won the Calder and shared the Art Ross with Dionne.

This magnificent rookie could have won the "Grand Slam."

"I have mixed emotions about the other two trophies," admitted Gretzky, on the day he was told of the

Gretzky magic keeps him healthy
(BRIAN GAVRILOFF, EDMONTON JOURNAL)

two he did win. "I understand that when the Art Ross Trophy was awarded, it was stipulated by the Ross family that they wanted one winner. But when Bobby Hull and Andy Bathgate tied, the owners should have had a vote. I hear they are talking about splitting the trophy in the event of a tie in the future. And they should. I don't think it's right the way it is. I have younger brothers and they have a lot of friends and they've all been brought up to believe an assist is just as important as a goal. The kids are having second thoughts about that now. The kids don't believe that any more.

"As for the Calder, I was disappointed about that. But I have to admit that I did know when I signed with the WHA, that it would be that way. I can't blame anybody but myself and, to some extent, the league because they didn't recognize the WHA a couple of seasons earlier."

And as for the Hart and the Lady Byng, Wayne Gretzky was saying, "One is just as nice as the other. Maybe someday we'll win a Stanley Cup to put between the two."

A tough act to follow

It would, everyone agreed, be a tough act to follow. After winning the Hart Trophy and the Lady Byng, and ending up tied for the scoring title with Marcel Dionne at 137 points in your first season in the National Hockey League, what do you do for an encore?

"I thought about the 137 points and the awards over the summer," The Kid confessed when he showed up at his second NHL training camp.

"Maybe I put a knife to my own throat.

"I guess I've made it tough on

myself. You know the old saying: 'If you score two goals, they want three.'"

Still, Gretzky hadn't changed his tune.

"I feel a lot stronger now that my tonsils are out. I'm really looking forward to this year. I think we have a lot better team now, and I have more desire to get going than I ever had. I still have a lot of things to prove. There are still a few doubters. I see, for example, that Marcel Dionne has changed his tune. He was quoted in *The Hockey News* as saying I won't have proved myself until I've been in the league for five years."

As a 19-going-on-20-year-old, Gretzky said his ambition was "to score one more goal than Marcel Dionne" this season.

Although some people were talking of Gretzky as a one-year-wonder, the majority were viewing him as a legitimate great now And some were even asking him if he were the best player in the NHL.

"Guy Lafleur is the best player in the league," said Gretzky. "Someday I hope to be."

If he wasn't about to surpass Lafleur as the best player in the game in 1980-81, he was certainly about to close any gap there might have been between the two.

It becomes more difficult now to remember that Gretzky was only 19. For instance, when Oilers' media guide came out, 20-year-old rookie Glenn Anderson listed 19-year-old Gretzky as his "childhood idol."

Canada's Male Athlete of the Year

As the season progressed, any doubts about Gretzky being a one-year-wonder had disappeared.

And, in the annual Canadian Press year-end poll, Gretzky was named Canada's Male Athlete of 1980.

Gretzky—who had also won the Charlie Conacher Award which goes to the NHL player who makes an outstanding contribution to humanitarian or community service projects—was an overwhelming choice over Terry Puhl of Melville, Saskatchewan, an outfielder with the Houston Astros of baseball's National League.

And, unlike the year before, when Gretzky was getting NHL players' autographs for his kid brothers...

One night when the New York Islanders were in town, goaltender Chico Resch asked Gretzky for his autograph.

"It's for my 15-year-old nephew," he told Gretzky. "He didn't want my autograph. He wanted yours."

The Leafs for Gretzky, and Moncton, too

In the first half of the season, there were those who were saying Gretzky wasn't having the year he had had in 1979-80 but, by the time the Boston Bruins and Toronto Maple Leafs had visited Edmonton in early January, the critics had been silenced—again.

Gretzky had been involved in 10 of the 11 goals the Oilers scored in the two-game series. In the previous year, after 40 games, Gretzky had 58 points. After the Boston and Toronto visits, the Oilers had played 37 games and Gretzky had 60 points.

Leafs' owner Harold Ballard made the trip to Edmonton to watch Gretzky do his usual number on the Leafs.

"I'd trade my whole team for Gretzky," said Ballard. "And I'd throw in Moncton, too.

"I might as well trade my whole team for him. If I got him, I'd have nobody to play with him anyhow."

Funny. That happened to be the Oilers' problem. They hadn't had anybody to play with Gretzky either. So far in the season Gretzky's wingers had been Dave Semenko, Don Murdoch, Brett Callighen, Jari Kurri, Blair MacDonald, Mark Messier, Glenn Anderson and Don Ashby.

"Gretzky has had a new winger just about every game," admitted coach Sather. "Every day, my number one priority as general manager is to find a goal scorer for Gretzky. We have to put somebody on that line who can score, and score every night. If I could find somebody, either in a trade or in the draft, who could score 50 or 60 goals, it would be heaven. The only thing I worry about in the meantime is that I'm going to burn him out."

Callighen and Kurri would end up as Gretzky's regular line-mates the rest of the way. And as the season progressed, it would become a trifle obvious that he was having a much better season. Much better than anybody in hockey history.

Gretzky fit to be tied –with Marcel Dionne

The Oilers were in Quebec City when they completed the first half of their schedule. A five-point night from Gretzky had just propelled the Oilers to a 6-3 win over the Nordiques.

"Why do I think I've been down this road before?" said Gretzky after the game.

The five points left Gretzky tied with Dionne at the half-season mark, each with 70 points. But Dionne had 10 more goals, so he won the half-season scoring race and the $500 prize money.

"After 120 games, I have the same

number of points as Dionne, yet I've lost two scoring titles."

A couple of weeks later, it was obvious that this would not be the case after 160 games.

First, the Oilers, led as always by Gretzky, scored what everybody was convinced would be the win of the year for the team. It was one of the most impressive "defeats" in the entire history of the greatest team in the history of hockey. The Oilers hammered the Montreal Canadiens 9-1.

"It was the thrill of a lifetime to beat Montreal 5-3 last year," said Gretzky, who led the way scoring five points.

"From a fan's point of view, "that has to be the biggest win we've ever had."

The Kid was rolling now. And exactly one month after the midway mark of the schedule, Gretzky finally passed Dionne.

Three goals and three assists against the Winnipeg Jets put Gretzky three points up on Dionne.

The gap would widen.

Making a move on the record book

Nobody had been mentioning it before, but now it was being noticed. The Kid had a shot at a couple of records that many people believed would never be broken.

In 1970-71, Bobby Orr recorded 102 assists. At his current pace Gretzky would end up with 104 assists.

And points? The record was Phil Esposito's 152 from the same season. Gretzky would end up with 151 if he kept scoring at his incredible rate.

Gretzky, who had been avoiding comment on the scoring race all season, was inspired to admit a few things after the Winnipeg game.

The Orr record, he said, fascinated him.

"If I'm ever going to break a record," he said, "that would be the one I'd want. I consider myself a playmaker more than a scorer. I don't consider myself a natural scorer."

And as for the scoring race?

"It will be different from here on in," predicted Gretzky. "Last year I played catch-up all the way in the scoring race. Now that I'm ahead, I think it will be easier on me."

But the scoring championship and records were not the only thing Gretzky had a shot at. He had a chance to win the Hart Trophy again. And by February 18th, when the St. Louis Blues came to Edmonton, it was more than obvious the battle for the Hart Trophy was down to two — Gretzky and St. Louis netminder Mike Liut.

Gretzky vs. Liut was obviously the way the game would be billed. And if one game can affect the voting for a season of play, this one did.

Gretzky played what many observers called his second or third greatest game in the NHL.

Five goals!

And two assists!

While setting Oiler NHL records for most goals in a game and fastest two, three, four and five goals in a game, Gretzky also tied a National Hockey League record for most goals in a single period — with Busher Jackson.

"Busher Jackson?" asked the 20-year-old. "Who is that? He must have broken in before Gordie Howe, eh? I've never heard of 'The Busher'."

Gretzky was only one goal shy of equaling the NHL record of six goals in a game. If he had done it, he would have done it in front of the man who set the record, St. Louis coach Red Berenson.

"I remember Berenson getting that record," said The Kid. "I was eight that year. I was playing novice hockey then. But I remember it."

Watching that game was enough for one Hall of Famer to wave the white flag.

Goaltender Glenn Hall watched from the press box and when it was over he said he thought he'd faced the best, but now he knew one had come along who was better.

"Wayne Gretzky is the greatest hockey player I've ever seen," said Hall that night.

The Oilers beat St. Louis 9-2, and Gretzky now led Dionne 112-105. And one couldn't help but think back to Walter Gretzky's prediction at the all-star game.

"He'll win by 22 points," said dad.

With 23 games to play, Gretzky needed 40 points to equal Esposito's record and 28 assists to equal Orr's.

"It's going to be close," said Gretzky after the game.

Gretzky chasing the records — that would obviously be the story-line for the rest of this season.

Pleau sparks new-line great debate

Unfortunately for a day or two, there would be controversy about the record.

In Hartford, on March 26, the Oilers scored three empty-net goals and won 7-2 as the Whalers tried in desperation to score with a sixth attacker and improve their dismal chances for a playoff spot. Gretzky, who earlier in the game was credited with an assist, scored one goal and added two more assists with the Whaler net empty. This sudden out-

Close-in action against the Whalers
(BRIAN GAVRILOFF, EDMONTON JOURNAL)

burst gave him 151 points, now only one point behind Esposito's record.

In Boston, general manager Harry Sinden called it "a farce." He said, "I don't think it was proper," and added, "I hope it doesn't detract from young Gretzky's accomplishment."

Minnesota North Star coach Glen Sonmor said he had serious questions about the move by Pleau to leave the goaltender out with the score 5-2 and then 6-2. "Somebody should be asking Pleau about his reasoning."

However, the man whose record stood to be broken said, "Big deal. He's going to get the record anyway. Over an entire season things even out and these sorts of things happen a lot."

Gretzky? He was avoiding all controversy.

"Any time you come close to any records of any sort," said Gretzky, "it's on your mind. Considering it's Esposito's, I'm honored to be coming close to him. I was only eight or nine years old when he was going good."

The Oiler center was scoring at an unprecedented 2.01 points-per-game clip. And everybody was converging on Detroit to watch him break it the next time out. "I've got three tickets for my mom, dad, and little brother," said Gretzky, "and there are a lot of other people that I know who are driving down to see the game."

Wayne Gretzky: King of the NHL

Gretzky tied Esposito's record in Detroit with a pass to Risto Siltanen in a 4-2 win over the Red Wings. The following evening in Pittsburgh he assisted on goals by Mark Messier, Brent Callighen, and Jari Kurri in a game that the Oilers won 5-2. The three assists not only helped Gretzky clear the Esposito record with a whopping 155 points, but gave him 102 assists which tied him with Bobby Orr for the most assists in a season.

"I'm happy and relieved to get it over with," said Gretzky, who had surpassed Esposito with a 24-point spree in his past ten games (20 assists, 4 goals).

Gretzky had said before the season that all he wanted to do was improve on his 137 points of the previous year, but he did have a distant goal in mind: "I wanted two points per game if I could get it because no one has ever done that before."

In the Oilers' 78th game, a 4-4 tie with Colorado, Gretzky got the one point he really wanted, the one that broke the supposedly impossible-to-break assist record of Bobby Orr. Gretzky set up Jari Kurri twice in the game to do it.

Orr played 78 games with Boston in the 1970-71 season to establish his assists record. Gretzky surpassed Orr in the same number of games and had picked up 22 assists in the past nine games to do it. Wayne said, "I really wanted to do it tonight so that nobody could complain I had done it in more games."

The Oilers finished the season off by hammering the Winnipeg Jets 7-2 to finish in 14th place and Gretzky wound up with the best individual season of all time with a goal (number 55) and four more assists for an incredible 164 points. That's 12 more points than Esposito, 7 more assists than Orr, and his average points per game worked out to 2.05. And Dionne was 29 points back.

Gretzky actually bettered his father's prediction at the all-star break when he led Dionne by only four points.

"I would never have bet on me getting that many points," admitted Wayne. "I really thought the team could finish where we did. You have to improve a little bit each year . . . next year it will be tenth place."

The youngest player before Gretzky to win the NHL scoring title was Busher Jackson who won it at the age of 21 in 1931-32. Busher had 28 goals and 25 assists for 53 points in 48 games.

Gretzky earned 94 points in the second half of the season surpassing the record of 87 set by center Stan Mikita of the Chicago Black Hawks in 1967-68, the season the NHL went from six to twelve teams.

"If Wayne Gretzky is not the league's most valuable player again, the guys picking them are retards," said Oiler coach Glen Sather. "Wayne Gretzky is the best thing hockey has seen in the last decade."

"They play with no nerves."

The voting for the NHL awards wouldn't be announced until June and it was now on to the playoffs for Gretzky and the Oilers. If there were any doubters left after the regular season, Gretzky took care of them in the first game of the Stanley Cup playoffs.

It was in the Montreal Forum. And against the Montreal Canadiens in what some people believed might have been Gretzky's greatest game. There had already been so many it was tough to say. Five assists to tie a Stanley Cup record. Three assists in the first period to tie another one.

To everyone Gretzky was the story. But The Kid pointed to the corner of the dressing room and correctly labelled Andy Moog as *the story*.

Coach Glen Sather had taken a gamble and started a kid named Andy Moog in goal, and The Kid at center was marvelling at his overnight co-star.

"Honestly," said Gretzky, "Andy Moog is the most confident 20-year-old I've ever met."

Moog, who broke into the NHL by allowing a goal on the first shot he faced fourteen weeks earlier in Los Angeles, flipped and flopped and stopped twenty-eight of thirty-one shots as the Oilers won 6-3 and took game one of the best-of-five preliminary series.

When the Oilers won the NEXT game 3-1, there was shock in the face of every fan who was there. Those faces were different from the year before when the Minnesota North Stars won three games in the Forum and knocked the Canadiens out of the playoffs in the second round. It was disbelief when Minnesota did it: shock and horror was more the way to describe them this year.

The Oilers were still children. Didn't they realize who they were playing? Didn't they understand?

The Oilers had not been intimidated by the rink, by the uniform, by the history, or by anything.

"They play with no nerves," said Canadiens' coach Claude Ruel.

The Gretzky and Moog Show

The scene that greeted the Oilers when they arrived home for game three at the Northlands Coliseum was one they would not soon forget.

On one side of the Coliseum hung a sign that read: "We believe in miracles." On the other side sat a fan in a Montreal Canadiens' jacket with a bag over his head. Between the two it said it all, if you *could* say it all about what had happened to the Oilers and to Edmonton in a span of four days.

And when the Oilers won game three 6-2 to sweep the series that night, you could have called it one of the greatest upsets in Stanley Cup history — maybe The Greatest Upset when you consider it was a 14th place club, a team of mere children, a club only two years out of the World Hockey Association. . . The team they beat was more than a third-place club; it was the legendary Montreal Canadiens.

Hard knocks by the Stanley Cup champs

When the Oilers arrived in Uniondale, New York, the first thing they noticed was that only one Stanley Cup pennant hung from the ceiling, not twenty-two.

But it was the most recent pennant, and the Islanders, according to a headline in the *New York Post*, did not like Wayne Gretzky's attitude coming off the Montreal series.

ISLES HOPE TO MAKE GRETZKY EAT HIS WORDS

screamed the largest sports headline in the edition. The article underneath it quoted Gretzky as having said, "We had to beat the best team in hockey to get here."

"That ticks me off," Bob Nystrom was quoted in the *Post*. "If he considers Montreal the best team in hockey, we'll just have to go out there and show him he's wrong."

"It's always good to hear somebody say that," Stephan Persson was quoted as saying. "The Canadiens were the greatest team in hockey but not now. I think Gretzky's got it backwards."

Gretzky cuts around a sprawling Paul Shmyr and dekes North Star goalie Don Beaupre
(BRIAN GAVRILOFF, EDMONTON JOURNAL)

For openers, the Oilers lost 6-3 and 8-2 to the Islanders. But back home on Easter Sunday, it was the Oilers' official day of confirmation. The Oilers won 5-2 and for the moment were back in the series.

And once again, this was a study. For the Edmonton Oilers this was the most memorable moment in their history.

"With the Montreal series, and so far in this series, I'd say we have matured at least a full year as a hockey team in a span of less than three weeks," said Gretzky, who scored his second hat trick in the playoffs to inspire the victory.

The Oilers were outstanding again at home in game four, taking the Islanders into overtime. The defending Stanley Cup champions avoided going home tied at two games with a sudden-death goal by Ken Morrow.

When the fans left the Coliseum after game four, they felt it finally had to be over for those Cardiac Kids. Surely they had run out of miracles.

The Edmonton Boys Choir

When the series returned to Uniondale for game five, it was abundantly clear that there had never been a team in the Stanley Cup playoffs quite like *this* one.

Four minutes remained in game five and the Edmonton Oilers sitting on the bench were singing. *Singing!*

"Here we go Oilers, Here we go... Here we go... Here we go Oilers, Here we go."

"Every time we got in trouble, we started singing," said coach Glen Sather, shaking his head.

"Teenagers," marvelled assistant coach Billy Harris.

If singing on the bench wasn't enough, they were also singing in their dressing room between the second and third periods.

"I think it was Mark Messier who started it," said Paul Coffey. "It just felt right to start singing. We don't know how to be goodie-goodies yet. We're a young team. We don't know how to sit there and take it all in stride."

What had happened was indeed unbelievable. A second-year NHL team. Seven players young enough to be playing in the junior Memorial Cup. Upsetting the Montreal Canadiens in three straight! Two wins in the Montreal Forum! And now a win on The Island! And taking the Stanley Cup champions to a sixth game...

The Oilers were outshot 23-12 in the last two periods, but Moog was spectacular and the Oilers won it 4-3.

"What it comes down to," said Gretzky, who set up two more goals for his 19th and 20th points in eight playoff games, "is that we're just going out there and trying to work as hard as they do. We're trying to be just as physical as they are. I know I've never been hit this much in my life. It's just amazing how loose we are, considering we're down 3-2. It's proof of what everybody is saying. We're too young to know what pressure is. We're the youngest team in the NHL. Just a bunch of kids. And what we're doing is saying to ourselves: 'Let's just give it our best shot.' It's wrong to say we're going to beat them. And we're not going to say that. All we're saying is that we've got nothing to lose. We're going to go back out and give it our best shot again."

As Gretzky spoke, from out of the

showers came the song again.

"Here we go, Oilers, here we go . . ."

Midnight finally comes for Cinderella Oilers

Back in Edmonton for game six, the Islanders prevailed and won what would prove to be their only tough series on the way to a second straight Stanley Cup.

The Oilers were out of the Stanley Cup playoffs. But for most Canadian hockey fans this year, Gretzky, Moog, and the Oilers MADE the Stanley Cup playoffs.

And unlikely as it may sound, the Islanders, too, had been captivated with the Oilers. It was a mutual admiration society in the dressing rooms when it was over.

While the mob of reporters interviewed coach Al Arbour in the hall outside the visitors dressing room, the Islanders, with big grins on their faces inside the room, began to sing a revised edition of the Oilers' hit song from the game before.

"Here we go Islanders, here we go . . ."

Wayne Gretzky, who ended with seven goals and 14 assists for 21 points in nine playoff games — the highest total of any player who didn't make it to the Stanley Cup final, and the only player who played less than ten games to score more than 12 playoff points — was left to put it in perspective.

"The most important thing we did was to create a winning attitude here," he said. "The Edmonton Eskimos don't know how to lose. We lost the series, but hopefully we also lost, forever, the droopy kind of attitude we had. Hopefully we'll start

to show a lot more in the regular season from now on. We didn't play intense hockey during the season. Now, when a player comes to this team, he'll have to adopt the attitude that is here."

Midnight finally came for Gretzky, Moog, and the Miracle Oilers of the 1981 Stanley Cup playoffs. But the sun would shine on them all summer.

The Kid's all Hart again — MVP 099

About the time it was being announced that Gretzky had been named Hart Trophy winner as the NHL's Most Valuable Player for the second year in a row, a set of licence plates were being placed on a 1961 Cadillac convertible.

The licence number: MVP 099.

Jeff Landry of Morinville, Alberta, had spent three years reconditioning the car, the exact length of time Gretzky had been in Edmonton. Only a couple of weeks earlier, Landry registered the Caddy. And finally, he was putting the plates on it — the very day Gretzky was named MVP.
when somebody noticed.

"Somebody in my shop brought it to my attention," he said of the plates which were regular issue. "I didn't even know what I had. I think it looks pretty good on the car. After all, 1961 was the year Wayne was born. And he most certainly is a Cadillac."

At 42 Varadi Avenue in Brantford, Walter Gretzky laughed.

"I know you are going to think I'm crazy, but I'm convinced Wayne's life was planned a long time ago. The things that have happened . . .

"A guy in Edmonton draws an MVP

099 licence plate number and puts it on his car, a Cadillac from the same year Wayne was born, the same day Wayne wins the MVP. . .

"It's like when Wayne tied Phil Esposito's record at 1:52 of the period and it was exactly 1:52 P.M. in Edmonton when he did it.

"I'm not even surprised at any of that stuff anymore. I really am convinced his life was planned a long time ago."

One thing that was planned a long time ago was that Wayne was going to let his dad keep all his awards.

"Even when I'm 40, they'll still go to my father," said Wayne. "I think he's more proud of them than I am."

The Kid, The Flower, and the Canada Cup

While all of this was going on, there was planning for the Canada Cup. And early in summer, people were beginning to speculate, as one headline put it, that there might be "Flower Power for The Kid?"

Gretzky was trying to be non-committal when people asked him who he wanted to play with in the Canada Cup.

"Um, oh . . . it doesn't really matter," he said.

But in the next breath somebody would mention the name Guy Lafleur and Gretzky would have a direct question to deal with.

"Well, I'd be honored if I got the chance to play alongside The Flower," Gretzky would say. "I guess I'd love to play with Guy Lafleur for sentimental reasons. It's just like when I got to play with Gordie Howe against the Soviets a few years ago."

On August 10th, for openers at least, Gretzky and The Flower were on the same line.

Team Canada coach Scotty Bowman made the announcement as training camp opened.

"Gretzky will play with Lafleur and Steve Shutt," he said.

Lafleur reacted with a smile.

"It will be a lot easier to play with him than against him. I've watched him play and I think he's a great hockey player. It will be great to have a chance to play with him."

When Team Canada arrived in Edmonton to play the Soviets in their final exhibition game, after much line juggling along the way, it was Gretzky, Lafleur, and Gil Perreault.

And the scene was magic in the Northlands Coliseum.

Gretzky's new line-mate was welcomed like he never expected.

All night the fans — who had occasionally booed Lafleur in the past, as fans will do to great hockey players who play for the visiting teams — chanted "Guy, Guy, Guy."

"I didn't expect that," said Lafleur. "Maybe it's the Edmonton fans' way of saying thank you for what happened last spring."

Gretzky with Lafleur was a dream.

"Wayne is doing everything," said Lafleur after Team Canada won the game. "Gilbert and I are still rushing things. We don't have good timing yet. Tonight, with the right timing, I could have had three of four goals set up by Wayne. I've never played with anybody who can do what he can do. When he's behind the net, it has to be tough on the Russians. They've never played against anybody who plays the game he does from behind the net."

After one look at Gretzky with his Team Canada team-mates, his regular season coach, Glen Sather, was prepared to make a prediction about how it was going to be.

"I think I wondered if he'd find his

Wayne, in full flight, releases a pass.
(BRIAN J. GAVRILOFF, EDMONTON JOURNAL)

level in the Canada Cup," said Sather. "Everybody saw it tonight. He was head and shoulders above anybody else on the ice. After watching him tonight, I don't have any doubt about him finding a level now. I think it's going to be his show."

It was already his show. Wayne Gretzky was everybody's cover boy for the Canada Cup. It was his Canada Cup and whatever happened, yea or nay, it was going to be that way.

The first major setback of a career

For the most part, it was yea.

Gretzky was the top point-getter in the entire tournament. Twice, in the game against Sweden and in the game against Russia, he won Labatt's soapstone carvings as Team Canada's Most Valuable Player.

For the most part it was magic.

But in the end...

In the end, the Soviets won the final 8-1.

Wayne Gretzky, like almost all of his team-mates, did not play well. He was, in the end, a Canada Cup goat. He wasn't there when it counted. And who would ever forget the fifth Soviet goal? Gretzky gave the puck away at the Soviet blue line. Guy Lafleur shied away from a fake shot and could only watch as the Soviet swept around him for a clear path to the net. And it was as though goaltender Mike Liut wasn't even there for the shot. That one goal summarized the entire evening.

"It was a strange feeling," said Gretzky. "You wanted to look at it as just another hockey game. But there was no way to rationalize the feeling that you let the whole country down. I just went and hid for five days. My parents didn't even know where I went."

Gretzky said the experience was probably good for him.

"It was the first real setback of my career," he said. "Everything in my lifetime has gone my way. Everything has gone well.

"It proved I have a lot to learn. But I'm only 20 and I'm sure I'll have another Canada Cup.

"I don't believe I'll have to spend 80 games trying to live down the one game in the Canada Cup. I think people finally believe I can play in the NHL."

In close vs. the Red Wings.

(BRIAN J. GAVRILOFF, EDMONTON JOURNAL)

The Greatest Single Season in Hockey History

s the 1981-82 regular season began, Wayne Gretzky called his shot. "I think it's time I started shooting more," he said, during training camp. "I think it's time to go for more goals. The teams are starting to get wise to me. They figure that nine times out of ten I'm going to pass."

The result? The greatest single season performance in hockey history.

Only three players — Mike Bossy, Marcel Dionne, and Charlie Simmer — managed to score more goals than Gretzky when he came up with 55 the previous season. But the revealing statistic was that Gretzky was way down the list, in 17th place, when it came to shots on goal in 1980-81.

"I must have learned something from watching Guy Lafleur for five weeks during the Canada Cup," he said, as he went through the pre-season schedule scoring two goals for every assist. "My shot seems to be harder and my release is quicker. And the goals are going in..."

Notoriously (if that word applies to a 20-year-old kid) a slow starter, Gretzky made the new game-plan work. By the 14th game of the season, he had 15 goals and 14 assists as compared to 5 goals and 11 assists after 14 games in his first NHL season, and 7 goals and 16 assists by game 14 in his record-smashing second season.

And as Gretzky goes...

The Oilers came out of the gate in great shape. In their first ten games it seemed obvious that the beautiful butterfly—which had emerged from the cocoon against the Montreal Canadiens and New York Islanders in the Stanley Cup playoffs the previous year—had learned to fly a regularly scheduled service in the National Hockey League.

Led, as always, by Gretzky, the Oilers' statistics said they were for real, as they visited New York during World Series week to meet the back-to-back Stanley Cup champions, the New York Islanders, for their first meaningful test. They were 7-3 in the win-loss columns and were leading the Smythe Division by six points going into the game. And they'd scored more goals than any other team in the NHL.

Their numbers were sensational. Five Oilers were in the top twenty in the individual points race. And the way they played in the first 37 minutes and 17 seconds in the game against the Islanders, out-shooting the champs 13-2 in the first period... well, the fan seated just below the press box was absolutely right: "They all look like Gretzkys," he said.

But by 7:17 of the second period, the question as to whether the Oilers had really "arrived" had been replaced by a bigger question: "Had this team come far enough to be able to survive without Gretzky?"

At 7:17 of the second period, it seemed as though that inevitable moment was at hand. You see, Billy Smith, the most aggressive goaltender in the NHL, had swung his stick and left Gretzky crumpled on the ice. Gretzky tried to return for a couple of shifts, but it was obvious he was hurt. He did not return for the third period.

Sitting in the stands, Oilers' owner Peter Pocklington had to think hard about the situation. Prior to the game, the Islanders had announced the signing of Mike Bossy for a reported $4.5 million for the next seven seasons. Not to be outdone, Pocklington had told Edmonton reporters that he'd reached an agreement with Gretzky on a renegotiated contract.

"It's a very nice contract," said Gretzky of the yet-to-be-signed deal. "The figures are tremendous."

The figures, many guessed, would be in the million-dollar-a-year range. And that was a lot of money to pay a player until 1999... especially if that player were to be injured and could no longer play.

With Gretzky out of the game in question, the Oilers fell apart. They were outshot 16-5 in the third period and lost the game.

Coach Glen Sather was of two minds: "Wayne not being there obviously contributed to what happened to us," he said. "But for the first time, despite what we saw in the third period, I honestly think we'd be strong enough to at least survive without Wayne. I wouldn't want to try it. But for the first time, I think we could."

Gretzky returned the next night in New York against the Rangers. "My dad always told me that pros are paid to play," Wayne explained. "I'm making good money and even though the injury was an aggravating one, I felt I had to try and play. I had to sleep with my leg bent, a string tied to keep it in that position. I skated in the morning before the game, went back to my hotel and put more ice on the knee. Then I came down to the rink at 4:30 for more treatment."

The bruise, on the muscle part of

the knee, was protected by a heavy bandage and a girdle.

"I figured if Joe Namath can wear panty hose, I can wear a girdle," he said.

It took him a period to get rolling. But he scored 2 goals and 2 assists, and would score 8 goals with 3 assists in his next three games. The thoughts of a Gretzky-less season were instantly replaced by the start of the most mind-boggling "Gretzky Watch" yet.

Gretzky and Oilers' palpitating pace

It seemed as if the season had hardly begun when people were asking Gretzky about the possibility of his breaking some of the game's most treasured records.

By November 4, the Edmonton Oilers had as many points in the standings as they had on December 20 the previous season. They were a full two months ahead of their 1980-81 pace in terms of wins, and had more points than any other team in the NHL. And when it came to Gretzky, as it always did, the thought was already beginning to occur to a great many fans: Fifty goals in fifty games.

"It's a little early to say I'm shooting for it," said the young man who had led his team to such dizzy heights with 15 goals in 14 games. "But I'm scoring more than I normally do."

Daily, the computations and calculations began appearing on sports pages around the country. Fifteen goals in 14 games. In his first NHL season, it took him until his 29th game to get his 15th goal. And in 1980-81 he didn't do it until his 32nd game.

Gretzky repeated his pre-season thoughts. "I was right about other teams figuring I'm going to pass 90 percent of the time. The goal I scored against Bunny Larocque the other night was a perfect example. Two guys went with Jari Kurri, so I just walked in. There didn't seem to be any sense in passing."

"He isn't behind the net as much," observed coach Sather. "Everybody knows that's his style and guys are hammering him back there. So he's moving in front more."

St. Louis netminder Mike Liut offered an interesting observation: "Bossy can score on you with a half dozen different deliveries. Gretzky isn't like that. And Gretzky's shot doesn't overpower you. But it almost never hits the middle of the net. Just the corners."

Lumley and Lady: thrill of a lifetime

Much had been made about the lack of quality wingers Gretzky has had to play with — Oiler tough-guy Dave Semenko being one — but there was the most unlikely of wingers on his line during a practice on November 6.

A female!

Mary Campbell, a 25-year-old Ottawa recreation department worker, was Gretzky's winger for fifteen minutes in a workout. It was for the CTV show "Thrill of a Lifetime."

"I've never skated with a girl before," said Gretzky.

"You've never done anything with a girl before," kidded Paul Coffey.

Gretzky, if he wasn't already getting used to an assortment of wingers, would soon see it as he'd never seen it before. He'd gone the early part of the season with Jari Kurri and Brett Callighen or Pat Hughes on his wing. But through early December he was largely teamed up with Dave Lumley and Dave Semenko.

The 50-in-50 streak was suddenly considered to be in definite danger.

On one hand the question being raised was, "How can anybody score 50-in-50 with Dave Semenko on one wing?", while on the other there was the matter of Lumley's scoring streak.

By November 29, Gretzky was now two months ahead of his goal-scoring pace from the previous year (up to February 13 and game 55). But he would not be on a goal-scoring binge in his next few games.

He went four games without a goal, but had 16 assists in that span — and the reason was Lumley's attempt at the modern-day record for scoring in consecutive games.

Lumley managed to come up one goal short of Charlie Simmer's modern-day record of 13, but along the way it was quite clear Gretzky was passing again instead of shooting.

"I'd really like Lummer to break the record," he said one night. "I'm certainly going to do everything I can to give him every opportunity to do so. This thing has kind of changed Lummer's whole life. Not only on the ice, but off. Everybody knows, now, about the attitude problem he used to have. What he is accomplishing has given him a great new attitude and he has a new confidence in himself on and off the ice that I think he's going to keep for a long, long time."

"Most of the thrill isn't the streak, so much as it is just to get the chance to play with Wayne," said Lumley, noting that Gretzky was five games ahead of the 50-in-50 pace until his record attempt came along.

"It's almost embarrassing," said Lumley. "It's like one of those quiz items. Which of the following names doesn't belong on this list: (a) Bobby

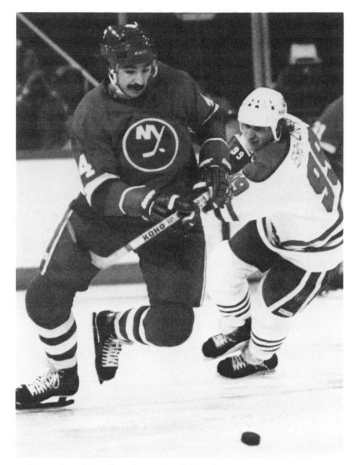

Forechecking hard vs. the Islanders.
(BRIAN J. GAVRILOFF, EDMONTON JOURNAL)

Hull (b) Andy Bathgate (c) Mike Bossy (d) Dave Lumley. Those are the three guys I passed when I scored in my eleventh consecutive game. But I have to be everybody's choice as the guy who doesn't belong.

"I can't help but wonder what the other players in the NHL are thinking. They've watched me play and I know they're all thinking, 'How in hell can Dave Lumley score goals in ten straight games?'

"I'm still not comfortable in this role. I'm not a goal scorer. I'm Dave Lumley, the guy who went 16 games without scoring a goal for the Nova Scotia Voyageurs. I'm the guy who spent 13 straight games in the press box earlier this year and it took two right wingers to get injured for me to get into the lineup."

Lumley was being honest with himself, with a little modesty thrown in for good measure. But he knew the score and even suggested that the record should probably be listed with the rest set by Wayne Gretzky.

"That's the kind of unselfish guy Gretz is. I've thought about the possibility that this record might be completely due to him. On one hand I tell myself it can't be, because he's only assisted on half the goals. But, at the same time, he's been on the ice for them all, and when he hasn't had the assists, he's been drawing guys away from me.

"I can't say for sure, but I really get the feeling he's going out of his way to try and feed me because of this. Especially early in the game. I'm getting a lot of chances early in the game. I think he wants me to get my goal early so he can go back to his regular game. But I don't know.

"All I know is that I head for the open spaces and I can count on the puck ending up on my stick. Playing with him you are guaranteed at least two great chances every game. I love playing with him. I don't know how to describe it. More than anything, I guess, it's fun."

Gretzky admitted the Lumley-Semenko combination put him into a feeder role instead of the scoring role he planned for himself at the start of the season.

"It's a little different," he said. "With Lummer and Semenk, I'm going to try to get them the puck. With Jari Kurri, Brett Callighen, or Pat Hughes, they got the puck to me a little bit more."

But with the end of Lumley's streak, things started to change. Every winger on the team was getting a chance to play with No. 99. He was being long-shifted and double-shifted.

"The inspiration," said assistant coach Billy Harris, "was that it prevented the other team from using a set line against Gretzky. Wayne has an extra minute or so of on-ice endurance that other players don't have. It gives us the opportunity to make the most of that as well."

"It's given me maybe six to eight minutes more ice time this year than I had last year," said Gretzky. "All I know is that I seem to thrive on extra ice time and longer shifts. For some reason, and I don't know why, when my body gets tired, I seem to do a lot better."

No lack of fresh, new angles and plots

The Boston sports media—which had had Bobby Orr to rave about a decade earlier—had warned the Edmonton sportswriters that they'd tire of having Wayne Gretzky to write about every day. Sooner or later, they suggested, there would be nothing left that hadn't been written before.

Maybe.

But not yet.

There had been no lack of fresh new scenarios. The most obvious new angle was the possibility of 50 goals in 50 games. It was early yet, but papers were now running daily thermometer-type charts to track his progress.

But there were plenty of subplots along the way.

On the night of December 13, with 1:02 remaining in game 32 against the Islanders in Edmonton, Gretzky scored goal No. 33 to remain ahead of the pace required to break Rocket Richard's record. But who would have expected to walk into the dressing room after watching the goal and hear Gretzky say: "That was probably the happiest I've ever been after a goal."?

One of the few remaining knocks on the now super-duper star was that he didn't score big goals. But this one was his fourth winning goal of the season. He'd only managed three the year before.

There was also the Lumley consecutive-games-scoring-streak plot, of course. And the statistical plots were endless.

By December 13, he was only two points shy of averaging two points per game for his *entire* NHL career. By this date he had 490 major league points (including WHA). At the start of the season he'd been considered a long shot to get 500 major league points by his 21st birthday, January 26. But he now had a shot at 500 before his 20th Christmas.

He also had a chance to score his 200th NHL goal during the season, and his 500th NHL point.

And even if he didn't get Rocket's 50-in-50, his chances looked excellent for Phil Esposito's record of 76 goals in a single season.

But the plot wasn't just thickening from a statistical point of view.

Awards, including Player of the Week, Player of the Month, Canada's Athlete of the Year, and many, many more had already become dime-a-dozen stuff for Gretzky. But it was not a ho-hum what-else-is-new item when *The Sporting News* named him its "Man of the Year." He'd become the first Canadian and the first hockey player ever to win that award.

Gretzky, Oilers owned Christmas

Wayne Gretzky's impact on the game was visible everywhere.

Like Christmas.

When most of today's adult fans were growing up in Canada, the routine was the same on Christmas morning. They would head to the rink to compare hockey related gifts. And every second kid was either wearing a new Montreal Canadiens sweater or a new Toronto Maple Leafs sweater.

But in 1981 it was obvious that when Santa Claus came to town anywhere in the country, he'd be carrying a bag full of Oiler items. Gretzky and the Oilers had become the grinches who had stolen Christmas in Canada from the Montreal Canadiens and the Toronto Maple Leafs.

"The term is probably 'phenomenal,'" said Jerry Sabourin, an executive with Grant emblems, the licenced manufacturer of NHL crests for Sandow hockey jerseys.

"The Oilers are out-selling the Canadiens and Leafs *combined* at least two to one. I've never seen a demand for any one team even remotely close to the demand for the Oilers. For every one Oiler crest that goes out, there's only one from all the other teams in the NHL combined that we're sending out right now. We can't keep up to the demand for the Oiler crest."

Sabourin figured the demand was "about 60 percent Gretzky and 40 percent Oilers," up from about 99 percent Gretzky and 1 percent Oilers from the same time the year before.

The Oilers were still leading the league and, as a result of their playoff performance the previous year, they were becoming almost as big a deal collectively as Gretzky individually.

"The general reaction from all the licenced suppliers is that they can't keep up to the demand for items with the Oiler logo on it," said Oilers' Director of Properties, Dan Fahey. "There are more than 200 items with the logos on them and every report we've received is that our logo has become No. 1."

'When,' not 'If'—
that was the question

The date circled on most calendars was January 16. Gretzky, his father, and his agent, Gus Badali, all said that's when they figured goal No. 50 would come. It was game 47. The Oilers were in Toronto.

By Christmas, Gretzky had scored 41 goals in 37 games. The projection seemed about right.

But it didn't work that way. Not even close.

The Los Angeles Kings were the first holiday visitors to the Northlands Coliseum on December 27. And if the record seemed two or three weeks away when they arrived, it seemed a whole lot closer when they left.

"It's like trying to throw a blanket over a ghost," Kings' coach Parker MacDonald said, after Gretzky—for the second time in the season against the Kings, and the third time overall—had a four-goal night. Two of his goals came with the Oilers short-handed. On one, he undressed defenceman Jay Wells. On the other, he scored on a breakaway. His others came on a quick dart from behind the net and on a rebound from the top of the crease.

The explosion gave Gretzky 45 goals and 102 points in just 38 games, and 403 career points in less than $2\frac{1}{2}$ NHL seasons.

And it gave him his first major record. He shattered the existing NHL record for fastest 100 points established by Phil Esposito eleven years earlier. Esposito took 51 games to reach the plateau en route to his 152-point season.

If there was any doubt that he was going to get the record, and get it long before he could do it in front of family and friends from Brantford at Maple Leaf Gardens, it had been erased.

"I sure hope he gets it before then," said assistant coach Harris at the time. "I want to get tickets in Toronto and right now I hear they're scalping them for about $200 each."

The new date circled on the calendar was January 2, a national Hockey Night in Canada game against the Boston Bruins in Edmonton.

The Oilers would play Philadelphia at home and Vancouver on the road before Boston came to town. Gretzky said it would be nice to do it against the Bruins, because he's enjoyed less success against Boston than any other team—and checker Steve Kasper, who was fast becoming his personal nemesis, had stymied him repeatedly.

"It would be nice to get it in Edmonton," said Gretzky. "I've been watching films of the Bruins for the past two weeks."

The Rocket concedes
Gretzky's greatness

The next, in the never-ending series of similar questions, was "How's The Rocket taking all this?"

Now there was absolutely no doubt that his record would fall.

"It's hard to believe," said Richard. "I started thinking about my record being equalled when the first expansion came, but I never thought it would be surpassed. And he's going to make it before his 42nd game!

"I've seen some good skaters— Beliveau, Schmidt, O'Connor—but they were never like Gretzky. He's a natural skater and every time he scores a goal, it looks easy. Everything he does looks easy. He plays everywhere. He's all over the place, so he's impossible to check.

"The game has changed. All the players think of now is shooting the puck and running after it. They don't hold onto it anymore. There are too many weak players on defence, too. That's why Gretzky is having so much fun now—the game is all offence.

"I think in a six-team league like there was twenty years ago, Gretzky, in spite of everything, would be the top scorer. He probably wouldn't score as many goals but he would prove beyond a doubt that he's a superior player."

The Rocket said Gretzky was a thing of the past in the present. He said Gretzky was playing the kind of hockey he, Richard, grew up with.

"He's great. There's no doubt about it," said Richard. "There's no way anyone will stop him from being the greatest star in hockey."

The other 50-in-50 man was handling it well, too.

"Gretzky isn't just anybody," said Mike Bossy, the New York Islander who tied Richard's feat the year before, "and this isn't the first record he'll break. He seems on course for a 100-goal season and I think he can do it."

Billy Harris had played against the Rocket while with the Leafs in the '50s and had the pleasure of watching the evolution of Gretzky as well.

"I don't care what anybody says about the difference in eras," said Harris. "I watched Gretzky the other night and I was just dumbfounded. We were tied 3-3 with the Islanders and it was a one-on-one situation. Gretz got by Denis Potvin and fired a shot past their goaltender (Billy Smith). I can remember The Rocket scoring the same kind of goals."

Harris viewed the difference in eras objectively enough.

"I think Wayne would be the first to admit that nowadays you're looking at about 63 different goaltenders, assuming some teams carry two or three," Harris said. "Prior to expansion you played every game against the six best goaltenders in the world. An example of that would be to look at Phil Esposito's production prior to expansion. It was nowhere near what it was after expansion. Back in The Rocket's day, players were much more familiar with the Rocket's style because they played each other fourteen times a season. It's not the same with Gretzky.

"I agree with The Rocket. Gretzky wouldn't have as many goals but he'd still be the scoring leader. He's an unbelievable playmaker. In fact, if he was a selfish hockey player, he'd have 60 to 65 goals right now."

The Rocket's red glare a mere flick of a Bic?

Wayne Douglas Gretzky, aged 20, wouldn't wait. If he was going to smash The Rocket's record, he wanted to smash it to smithereens.

Philadelphia Flyers were next up on the night of December 30, 1981, and it was a 7-5 win. But the score would hardly be mentioned in the media the next day. Nor would the fact that it was the Oilers' 25th win of the season and they were alone in first place overall in the 21-team league. And rookie goaltender Grant Fuhr's 19th consecutive win would go unpublicized as well.

For 17,490 fans in the Northlands Coliseum, it was a young man's dance with destiny—Gretzky vs. The Rocket and Mike Bossy.

The way it worked out, Gretzky left as little room as possible for anyone to ridicule the record because of expansion, the style of play, and all the other sacred excuses. It was more than just another Great Gretzky game.

To most who were there, it was the greatest hockey game ever played by the greatest player in the history of the game, to break the greatest record ever set in the game.

It was more than hockey history, it was magic. For most fans who were there, it was "The Game I'll Never Forget."

Five in one night. Nine goals in two games. Fifty goals in 39 games!

You could see the determination on his face from the cheapest seat in the house. And the crowd played the entire game with him. Seldom have so many fans gone through so much anguish with a player having the greatest game of his life. He'd already scored three, halfway through the

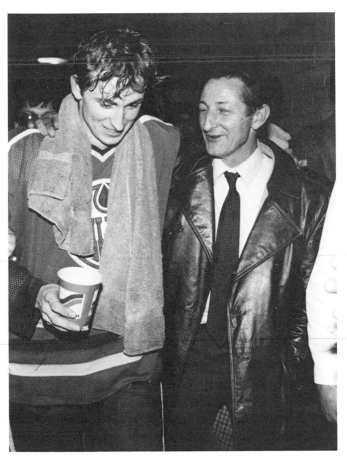

Wayne celebrates his goal-scoring record with his dad.
(BRIAN J. GAVRILOFF, EDMONTON JOURNAL)

second period, and the fans were so restless it was unbearable. When he scored No. 49, the crowd — which had long since come to expect the impossible — reacted like never before.

They'd chanted "Guy-Guy-Guy" for Guy Lafleur in Edmonton during the Canada Cup, and "Andy-Andy-Andy" for goaltender Andy Moog in the playoffs against the Canadiens the year before. But — unbelievable though it may seem — until that moment, they had never cheered "Gretzky-Gretzky-Gretzky."

"Any superlatives I might offer would be inadequate," said Flyers' coach Pat Quinn.

Pete Peeters, an Edmontonian, was in goal for the Flyers. "What he did was absolutely amazing," said Peeters, who was at least saved from going down in history as the man who gave up the record-setting goal. Gretzky scored it into an empty net with three seconds to play.

"This is absolutely crazy," said Flyers' captain Bobby Clarke. "At least with Bobby Orr, you'd see him wind up in his own end and you could try to set up some kind of defence to stop him. Gretzky. . . he just comes out of nowhere. It's scary."

"We take a lot of pride in the fact that we can force other teams to play our game," said defenceman Jimmy Watson, "that we can control a big guy like that with our zone defence. But I don't think anybody is going to stop him."

Gretzky scored the first one on a five-footer from the edge of the crease. The second came on a drive from 35 feet. The third was on a breakaway and the shot was from 25 feet out and went in off Peeters' chest. The fourth was a 30-footer over Peeters' shoulder.

It was the second time in his career he'd scored five in one game. He'd now scored in nine straight games.

Ignored was the fact that this night Gretzky had scored his 198th, 199th, 200th, 201st, and 202nd goals since turning pro in the World Hockey Association. Gretzky had 11 shots against the Flyers and also drew an assist in the game. The Kid had scored on 15 of his last 32 shots. After 39 games, Gretzky had already taken 174 shots on goal, only 90 fewer than he'd taken in the previous season. "Last year I would have passed on three of the goals I scored tonight," said Gretzky.

Two Oilers said they saw it coming.

"Things like this aren't supposed to happen," said Paul Coffey. "Yet when he sets a goal for himself, he gets it, it's that simple. He wanted to do it before the 40th game. You could have bet $1 million against him doing it, but I knew he would."

Gretzky's roommate, Kevin Lowe, also suspected the explosion might be coming. He said he knew it hours before the game when the two were sitting down to bacon and eggs (cooked by Wayne).

"He doesn't really say much about his goals," said Lowe, "but when I talked to him he said there was no reason why he couldn't score five against the Flyers."

Gretzky, of course, was not in much of a position to compare his record to The Rocket's because he wasn't born by 1944-45.

"I can't even remember seeing any six-team NHL games on TV," he said. "But I recall seeing The Rocket on a between-periods interview once.

"And I can say is that I believe hockey is better now than it was, say, fifteen years ago. I think the players are bigger and better. And fifteen years from now, I think they'll be bigger and better than we are. Everything improves."

Was it the greatest game he'd ever played?

Normally, Gretzky gave it the Dizzy Dean approach ("I'll score 'em, you rate 'em"), but on this night he was willing to rate 'em.

"I guess I'm more delighted with this than anything," he said.

"People are now going to have to reevaluate their stars of the century," said coach Sather. And then he added: "I still don't think we've seen the best of Gretzky yet."

The following night, Gretzky would close out the calendar year, and complete the first half of the regular schedule, by being blanked against the Vancouver Canucks on the west coast.

In the calendar year 1981, Gretzky scored 95 goals and added 142 assists for 237 points!

And where to, from here?

"I think I can double everything," he said. "As long as the rest of the guys on the team keep playing the way they are, I think I'm capable of doubling what I've done so far."

What he would do was one thing. What he had done that night was another. But what he did off the ice, after the game was over, was something else again.

"I was sitting at home listening to the radio, and the station was keeping us right up to date," said his father, Walter. "First they said he had 47 goals, then 48, then 49...I was really excited.

"Then he scored No. 50 and...

"Well, right after the game, Wayne called us from the dressing room. He said he just wanted to let us know what had happened.

"I want to tell you, when Wayne called, that accomplishment of 50 goals in 39 games meant absolutely nothing. Nothing at all compared to that phone call.

"Heck, he's a 20-year-old. He's a busy young man with all sorts of friends and plenty of things to do.

"There aren't many 20-year-olds who would take the time."

The road to Toronto

One hundred and thirty-two interview requests. That was for one guy. Throw in the rest and it was more than 200.

That was "This Week in the NHL" as the Oilers and their star attraction arrived in Washington, D.C. for the start of a four-game tour in early January which was, in effect, "The road to Toronto" for their one and only visit to Maple Leaf Gardens in 1981-82.

It was a Tuesday.

They were to play the Capitals on Wednesday and make their only visit of the season to Philadelphia—where the embarrassed Flyers waited for revenge—on Thursday, then play in Toronto, on Hockey Night in Canada, prior to finishing off the tour in Detroit on Sunday.

On Tuesday, Gretzky had to handle interviews from a battalion of media men, including an advance party of sportswriters from southern Ontario who were treating Gretzky's game in Toronto as the Second Coming.

The rest of the day Gretzky spent in a limousine with NHL president John Ziegler as they toured the local TV and radio stations to promote the NHL All-Star game, which was coming up a month later in Washington.

All Gretzky lacked in the tour through Washington, to make it strictly presidential treatment, were a couple of flags on the front of the limo.

By now, he was a media event.

A film crew shooting "A Day in the Life of Wayne Gretzky" was recording his every move. He was en route from one TV interview to another, doing a radio show on the telephone in the limousine, when he made a most favorable impression on the whole media multitude by holding up a single finger to say "Just one more minute"—giving the radio station every second he could even though he was only minutes from going on live at the next TV station.

There would be more media people waiting Thursday in Philadelphia, and there were so many people waiting to interview him Friday and Saturday in Toronto that Oilers' Public Relations Director, Bill Tuele, had to call a special press conference.

"We decided to have a two-hour press conference after practice on Friday so we could handle everyone at once," said Gretzky while in Washington. "I would have been interviewed in Toronto from just about the moment we landed until we took to the ice. I decided to go home to Brantford and spend some time with my parents and family after the press conference."

Although Gretzky had resorted to the press conference in Toronto, he remained amazingly accessible. One way or another, he managed to make time for everyone.

"He's the most patient guy I have ever seen," said Sather during the tour. "I know I don't have the patience. I had five interview requests for Tuesday when we got in here. One guy from Pittsburgh wanted to have dinner with me. I just don't have the time or patience to go along with that. And the stupid questions . . . I just don't have the patience to deal with them.

"But Wayne still answers everyone. He is still willing to accept it all as part of the game. But I don't know how much longer he can remain the way he is. After a while, when so many people demand a piece of your life . . ."

In the coming weeks that would hit home with Gretzky more than ever before.

One thing he'd certainly figured out was that playing in an off-the-beaten-path place like Edmonton certainly has its advantages.

"Edmonton is a blessing," said Gretzky. "I can find time for myself when I'm at home. I doubt if it would be like that in places like New York or Toronto."

But, again, it wasn't all Gretzky on the tour.

"In the past," observed Sather, "even at the start of this season, all the media was there for Wayne and only Wayne. But now other players are getting used to the idea that the people are becoming interested in them, too. Right now, Grant Fuhr is drawing media people who want to talk to him *before* they talk to Wayne. Paul Coffey, Kevin Lowe, Glenn Anderson, and Mark Messier—and Dave Lumley when he was on the goal-scoring streak—and to some extent everybody else, are getting a taste of it."

But never to quite the same degree.

Gretzky, everybody knew by now, could handle it. But the others?

"I'm not worried about them going on ego trips," said Sather. "There's no reason to believe they shouldn't continue to play as well as they did in the first half of the year. They've discovered now that they're as good as anybody in the league. My feeling is that they'll stay there."

Assistant coach Harris wasn't so sure. "I'm concerned that we could be getting complacent," he said. "With everything going on in this road trip . . . Well, it's going to be interest-ing to watch how everybody reacts."

The Oilers tied Washington 6-6 and were bombed 8-2 by Philadelphia. But their poor play in those games was understandable. They were caught looking ahead to Toronto themselves. The game had become more than just one of 80 regular season games. It was obvious, the way the game was being treated, that it was being viewed as The Game of the Year on Canadian soil.

'I feel like the Beatles'

Oilers' owner Peter Pocklington once threw out the quote: "Wayne Gretzky is to hockey what Pavarotti is to opera."

No contest.

The two went one-on-one in Toronto. Pavarotti tickets were only going for $150 a pair. Gretzky's were said to be averaging $250 a pair. And nobody offered $800 for a single ticket to Pavarotti as one fan was alleged to have advertised for Gretzky in Toronto.

And when it came to the media . . .

All week Gretzky had been treated like a rock star. Every time he stepped off a plane, bus or train, there had been at least one television film crew waiting to record the momentous event. It had been a media circus all week. But what had happened in Washington and Philadelphia had become a non-event compared to what he was met with in Toronto.

Never in the history of Canadian sports, many old-timers agreed, had there been such a reception for a Canadian athlete.

Some, such as Peter Smith, manager of the Westin Hotel, said it could compare only to a Royal Visit. "The only time I've seen anything that came close was when I was the manager of the Edmonton Plaza Hotel in 1978 and we had Queen Elizabeth and Prince Philip in the hotel for the Commonwealth Games."

Almost as many photographers, broadcasters, and writers in one room as are accredited each year for the Grey Cup game waited two hours for the flight-delayed arrival of The Great Gretzky. When he arrived, there was a twenty-minute question-and-answer period from the floor prior to a half hour of one-on-one interviews for the electronic media. During the question-and-answer period, one journalist desperate for a new angle— noting one of Gretzky's ancestors was from White Russia and another from Poland—asked him to comment on the Russia-Poland situation. Gretzky stickhandled his way around it.

The story wasn't anything that Gretzky said. The story was the scene itself.

"This scene is absolutely unbelievable," said Pocklington. "If you weren't convinced before, you have to be convinced now that Wayne has

Slick stickhandling undresses a Washington Capital.
(BRIAN GAVRILOFF, EDMONTON JOURNAL)

done more to put Edmonton on the map than all of the other 650,000 citizens of Edmonton combined."

"How can I complain?" said Sather. "Wayne deserves this. Wayne just proved again what a classy young gentleman he is. The kids today need somebody to idolize. I think it's better that they choose to idolize Wayne Gretzky than Mick Jagger."

Gus Badali said he never dreamed such a scene was possible. And he said he was moved by the way Wayne handled himself. "It's just like when he's on the ice. He doesn't get tired. He has some inner quality."

Gretzky's reaction? "I guess what happened to me here this afternoon is just about the greatest compliment ever paid to me," he said.

One particular incident said it all.

After the game in Toronto, in order to get Gretzky safely from the dressing room to the team bus, Dave Semenko and several Oiler officials had to play plain-clothes bodyguards. The exit and the team bus were surrounded by a mob of teenaged girls, screaming with delight just to get a glimpse of him and ecstatic if they actually managed to touch him.

"I feel like the Beatles," said Gretzky, in an embarrassed sort of way, as he worked his way down the aisle of the bus.

But as for the game . . . well, the Oilers bombed. They were abysmal. Goaltender Grant Fuhr ended his winning streak at 23 games. Gretzky managed to get a goal, but the final score was Leafs 7, Oilers 1.

And they went out, in front of a crowd of 20,628 on the coldest night in the year in Detroit twenty-four hours later, and bombed again.

Much ado about nothing.

"We should have realized this is how it would become sooner or later," said captain Lee Fogolin. "It wasn't that long ago when we were the club in 18th place and we were treating those games when the Montreal Canadiens came into our rink like it was the moon. Obviously we weren't prepared to handle it when it happened to us."

"I think we had been so successful that we got to the point where we started to believe that all we had to do was throw our sticks out on the ice," said Gretzky. "At the same time that was happening, we became kind of a trophy for other teams."

But, this time at least, the Oilers would snap out of it.

And so would Gretzky.

From Superkid to Superman?

When Gretzky signed his first contract to remain an Oiler until 1999, the fact that the year ended with the same number he wore on his back was a factor.

That deal was wiped out in January.

This time, the now about-to-turn-21-year-old signed for 21 years. Not entirely coincidental either. The first 15 years would be worth $20 million and would include a shopping center in Western Canada which would become his in 1988.

"Maybe Wayne will be a grandfather by the time the contract runs out," said Pocklington. "But that's fine. If Wayne doesn't play the entire 21 years, he'll have a job in our organization. You've got to remember that Wayne is the best hockey player in the world. If there's a God in it, he's it!"

"Whatever Peter pays him, it isn't enough," said Sather.

When Gretzky went out on his next road trip, the media in the U.S. who hadn't yet discovered him because of his age and his statistics, were now more than willing to discover him because of his new salary.

He arrived in St. Louis on his 21st birthday. And from that day onward—because of what he'd done and because he had become the Twenty-Million-Dollar Man—he would now have to be more than Superkid. He'd have to be Superman.

Now things would get serious, like the sign on the door to the room in the Marriott Hotel where Gretzky was officially pronounced *The Sporting News* Man of the Year. The sign read: "Due to a recent ruling by the Edmonton Oilers, Mr. Gretzky will not be granting any personal interviews this evening."

It would turn out that the sign didn't mean much. Gretzky this night would provide one of the most introspective interviews of his career.

The story-line was obvious. What was life going to be like for the Super-kid as an adult? He didn't paint a completely pretty picture.

"I can't go to a ball game and have a beer and a hot dog and be just like everybody else anymore," he said. "I can't be myself now. I can go to all sorts of private boxes, but I can't go sit in the stands and have a hot dog and beer."

His household name fame was no longer restricted largely to Canadian cities. "The change I've seen in the past year, heck in the past month, is a bigger change than I've seen in the last twenty years," he said.

He realized it was going to get worse. He realized that the demand on him had just begun. He realized that now he'd have to schedule his time completely, right down to the amount of time he would be able to allot to himself.

"In a lot of ways, the change is nice," he said. "I still enjoy being rec-

ognized and having people ask for my autograph. But there's so much of it. It's also frustrating."

And the changes were beginning to affect him. Suddenly he'd developed a fear of flying. "I admit it," said Gretzky. "I get scared on planes. I don't know what it is. I know I never used to be afraid. But there have been a few close calls in the last couple of years. Now I'm the happiest guy in the world when a plane finally lands. It doesn't bother me quite as much when I'm with a group. But when I'm flying around every day to fulfil my commitments in the summer, it really bothers me."

He was also developing a fear of crowds.

"You never know what can happen," he said. "You never know who is out there. When they start shooting the Pope, you start worrying."

The money itself, he realized, would make things different. The $20 million thing was already making it different. Half the questions at *The Sporting News* press conference were about money.

His "childhood" statistics, for the 1981-82 season, were 61 goals and 76 points or 137 points. His complete "childhood" record was 167 goals, 270 assists, and 437 points in the NHL. Including his year in the WHA, they were 213 goals, 334 assists, and 547 points.

"I guess what he does now is shoot for consistency, maturity, and leadership," said Oilers' coach Glen Sather.

Gretzky said his individual goal had always been to come up with one more point than he had the year before, but now he realized that would be impossible.

"The league has had such a change-over—there are so many young players—that if anybody ever gets 200 points in a season, it'll be in the next two or three years. I'm sure that as all the young players get experience, things are going to tighten up.

"The year when I don't outdo myself is bound to come. It has to come. And what happens then is one thing I know I'm going to face in my life. It's like Kevin Lowe told me the other day. If I get 200 points this year and only 170 the next year, I'll have to take a year away from the game so I'll have a chance to start over again. It was funny, and I laughed when he said it. But it's kind of true, too."

He admitted he'd been thinking about another thing. "I won't have a career which will last as long as Gordie Howe's or a lot of people. I know that now, too. I won't be able to keep playing when I'm getting 30 goals a year, instead of 50 or so goals a year. I won't be able to tell people my production is down but that I'm becoming an all-round hockey player. I'm paid to score goals and create plays."

There was one other question begging to be asked now that he'd reached adulthood. Would we soon be able to expect marriage and children?

"I know I've got the right girl to stand behind me. And I know she doesn't even care if I play hockey or not," he said of his girl friend, Edmonton singer Vicki Moss. "But she's 19 and we both have our careers and it's not the right time for either of us to get married."

"Besides," said his agent Gus Badali, "he has to give me one year's notice. I need a year to work a wedding into his schedule."

The Kid II troubled too

If Wayne was getting the idea that there were mountainous pressures ahead, he wasn't the only one.

Keith Gretzky was only 14, but, like his big brother, he had a head on his shoulders which seemed to have been around longer than the rest of his body.

While other kids his age were dreaming of one day playing with No. 99, Keith made up his mind that he'd rather play for twenty other teams before he'd want to play on the same team as Wayne.

"It's going to be tough enough on me if it turns out that I make it to the NHL," he said. "I don't want the comparisons that Dennis Hull had when he played on the same team as his brother Bobby.

"Already everybody expects me to be as good as Wayne. Because Wayne's there, I hope I'm not drafted by Edmonton."

That way he could wear his own No. 99, right?

"I'd like to wear No. 13," he said.

Not 99?

"Nah, he's got it.

"I'd like to wear 13 because the Russians have a 13 and I like the Russians."

Keith Gretzky, already a household name in Canada because of 7-Up commercials with his older brother, says there really shouldn't be many comparisons made between him and his brother.

"I think I play a different style than Wayne," he says. "I like a physical game. If somebody gives me a good, hard, clean check, I'll go out and make sure I give that guy a good, hard, clean check in return, except I make sure I hit harder.

"I'm a mean machine."

Gretzky goes to the White House

At the NHL All-Star Game in Washington, D.C., any comparison between Wayne Gretzky of the Edmonton

Oilers and Wayne Gretzky of the Campbell Soups was purely coincidental.

For the third straight year, Gretzky didn't wow 'em as an all-star. On the ice anyway.

"I'm always in a fog at the all-star game," he said. "But the idea is to have fun," he noted, and admitted that the night before the game he stayed up past midnight.

"For the other 80 games of the year, I've got pressure to produce. I decided I don't need to put that pressure on myself for the all-star game too. This is the one game of the year where I can forget about the pressure, where I can forget about all the shouting and screaming and just be one of the guys and go out and enjoy. This is the No. 1 fun game of the year and I come here to have fun."

Gretzky was speaking in the post-game Campbell Conference dressing room. Suddenly the man from *Izvestia*, the Soviet newspaper, burst into excited chatter to interpret the revelation into his tape recorder. Wayne burst out laughing.

"Don't get me wrong," he said in the direction of the Soviet scribe. "I care. We all care. We're here to show people that we're here for a reason. It's a showcase game so you want to look good and you hope everybody looks good. But you don't have the proper sleep or the proper routine.

"The all-star game is a reward. It's a chance to get to know all the other players in the league and to have an experience you're going to remember. I'll never forget the WHA all-star game because of what a thrill it was to play on the same line as Gordie Howe. And I'll never forget my first NHL all-star game because it was my first chance to get to know players like Guy Lafleur.

"I'm most certainly not going to forget this experience—meeting the President of the United States and Bob Hope...I was in a fog all day. I couldn't believe it was me sitting there at the White House with them. Even just being able to go inside the White House was a big thrill."

Oilers Grant Fuhr, Mark Messier and Paul Coffey were also picked to play for the Campbell Conference team in the youngest all-star game ever (there were twenty first-timers)— and the foursome raved.

Fuhr, the strong silent type, came up with his best (and only) line of the season when he remarked about meeting President Ronald Reagan: "I was even more stuck for words than I usually am."

Even Gretzky, who was getting used to rubbing shoulders with the famous in all walks of life, wasn't at ease in this situation.

"I kept looking at Gordie Howe and doing exactly what he was doing," said Wayne, adding that he had always followed any advice Gordie had to offer and this was no exception.

"I just told Wayne 'just pretend he's not there, finish your meal, and don't look up,'" said Howe.

Howe said he was invited so Reagan would have somebody his own age there to relate to. "He told me his dad took him to watch me play when he was a kid," said Gordie.

Gretzky was the only player mentioned in the President's speech.

"One of the latest sports heroes in this country is a modest young man from Ontario named Wayne Gretzky," said Reagan in prefacing the obligatory hands-across-the-border message. "We know that just north of the border there are so many fine people like him and we are happy to have them as neighbors and friends. That's what hockey and sportsmanship are all about."

The President also suggested that the Washington Capitals should give up two draft choices and the state of Texas to get Gretzky.

Gretzky, go get lost?

The controversy had been raging for weeks. Not whether or not Wayne would break Phil Esposito's single season record for 76 goals—that was assumed. The controversy was all about whether the Oilers would tell Gretzky to get lost for two weeks on some remote island as soon as he broke the record.

Assistant coach Billy Harris voted to send him to a remote hideaway and to hell with hockey history.

"As soon as he gets goal number 80, I'd send him away for eight or ten days," said Harris, after Gretzky notched goals 71 and 72 and points 157 through 161 on February 17 against Minnesota North Stars. "It's not my decision but I know how I'd handle it. I'd get him away. We've been kind of concerned the last three or four games about how tired he's looking. Until the second period tonight, he's looked pretty tired to us. What he did in the last two periods was the sensational stuff you almost come to expect from Wayne. We haven't seen him like that for a while."

It was an insane amount of pressure on Gretzky at this point. There he was, on the cover of *Sports Illustrated* for the second time in a season, on a 17-game point streak and only four goals shy of Esposito's record, and everybody was wondering, "What's wrong with Wayne?"

"People expect me to get four goals every game," he said, yet insisted he wasn't tired.

"I'm not tired. I'm frustrated. I just don't think I've played up to my abilities in the last couple of weeks, that's all."

Owner Pocklington went so far as to suggest that he and coach-general manager Sather had actually asked Gretzky to take a break, and not give the world of sport the full extent of the greatest single season in hockey history.

"We both went to him," said Pocklington. "But he says there's no way he'll do it. He doesn't think it would be fair to the team."

Not to mention the fans. And himself.

'Gretzky Watch' on again

Gretzky wanted to at least tie the Esposito record in front of the fans in Edmonton. He didn't quite do it.

In the final home game before an eight-game road trip, against Hartford Whalers, Gretzky needed four goals to tie Espo and...

And when the game was over Wayne was almost apologetic. "We play our last two games at home this year," he said. "If I score in either of those two games, that's the one the fans will remember. That will be the real record."

Gretzky "only" managed three goals and two assists against Hartford.

And at least one person in the Northland's Coliseum was relieved. Greg Millen, the goaltender of the Whalers.

For a while there, he was asking, "Why me?"

Millen used to be a friend of Gretzky's. Four years earlier they had been on the same junior team in Sault Ste. Marie.

"Greg used to pick me up in his car and take me to practice every day," remembered Gretzky. "We're pretty good friends. It's a small world after all, isn't it?"

"Too small," suggested Millen.

The previous season, Gretzky picked on Millen to score the then-historic 153rd point, to break

Esposito's single-season points record.

"I'm just glad he stopped at three," said Millen, imagining his name going into the record book and becoming an answer to a trivia question once again. "I was certainly aware every time he went on the ice. I knew he had a long way to go, but once he started putting them in . . . 'Oh, oh,' I thought. In the end, all I thought was 'thank goodness there isn't another period.'"

Esposito, Ziegler, wait for history

When the Oilers arrived in Detroit for game 63, they were met by Phil Esposito and NHL president Ziegler, who informed them they'd be travelling with the team until Gretzky scored the historic goal.

The Oilers said they'd been notified of that.

"Our instructions to Wayne are to go out and get a bunch of assists and no goals," said Billy Harris to Esposito. "We thought it would be nice if you could accompany us at least as far as Pittsburgh."

"Pittsburgh!" said Esposito. "I don't even want to go to Buffalo!"

A Detroit sportswriter predicted Gretzky wouldn't get the goal against the Red Wings: "I think he'd prefer to wait and score it against a *real* NHL team."

Gretzky compromised. He tied the record in Detroit.

For the record, Gretzky took a perfect relay from Glenn Anderson before beating goaltender Bob Sauve at 16:34 of the third period.

"Andy is noted for barrelling into situations," said Gretzky. "They paid attention to him and I think they forgot about me."

Gretzky scored 76 on exactly 293 shots. When Esposito established the record, he took a whopping 550 shots.

Esposito was delighted.

"I wanted to be here and I want to be wherever it is that he breaks it," he said. "I wanted to be here. When I broke Bobby Hull's record (58 goals), I wished he could have been there to see it. I was coming here whether the NHL said to or not. It's great what Wayne is doing for the game."

Seventy-Seven in Sixty-Four

So it was on to Buffalo. And the media circus would resume in full. Minus Gretzky—at least, until the last minute.

Gretzky went home to Brantford to visit his grandmother, to go to school classes with his kid brothers, and to see his commercial co-star and brother, Keith, play a minor league hockey game.

When he finally did show in Buffalo, he received the full treatment.

The world would be told that he ate cabbage rolls and borscht at his grandmother's, and watched the soap opera "One Life to Live."

He went to school and sat in on his brother Brent's grade-five class with the same teacher, a Mrs. Chiu, that he had as a young man 10 years old.

"A couple of kids in class did speeches on me," he said, a little bit embarrassed.

And in the game he watched, Keith had two shorthanded goals and four assists as Brantford beat Brampton 7-5 in the minor midget contest.

"It was the first time I'd watched Keith play in three years and he was great," said Wayne.

When he arrived for the morning skate on yet another date with history, Gretzky was relaxed and ready.

"I don't think I was nervous before

the game," said Gretzky, who was very much taking everything in stride, due to the fact he had known he would break this record for quite some time. "The only thing I felt anxious about was that Phil was here and I wanted to do it so he could get back to work."

As he'd almost made it a tradition, Gretzky didn't just settle for a single snipe for the historians. He doesn't break records—he annihilates them.

They came to watch him score No. 77. They saw him score No. 77, No. 78 and No. 79.

In goal was Don Edwards. He'd made a couple of great saves on Gretzky before the record goal went in.

The 77th was a 20-footer at 13:24 of the third period.

"When it went in," Gretzky told reporters, "the first thing that went through my head was 'that puts us ahead 4-3.' It was only when I made my turn that there was a sense of relief."

Esposito had been saving an anecdote for the moment.

Seven years earlier, Esposito said, he received a long-distance call from his dad in Sault Ste. Marie.

"Phil," his dad said, "there's a boy who will break all your records one day. He's 14 years old and he's playing junior in the Soo. His name is Gretzky. . . Wayne Gretzky."

"I remember saying, 'Well that's great, Dad, but he's only 14. Let's wait and see.'

"I had goose bumps for him," said Esposito. "Damn right I was excited."

So was Pocklington. "I was so excited sitting up there tonight that my wife Eva told me I love Gretzky more than I love her," he told Dick Chubey of the *Edmonton Sun*. "I told her not to push it."

Breaking out of a 'slump'

He'd already destroyed the two records in the season he would be most remembered for, but there were plenty to come. Gretzky, however, by mid-March, had found himself in a "slump."

"I see you've finally found the pipes again," his kid brother Brent said on the phone when Wayne broke a six-game scoreless streak.

"I've got a good family that way," said Wayne. "I remember going home after the season last year. I had 164 points and everybody was telling me how great I was and, when I got home, the first thing my dad said to me was, 'You should have had 175.'

"If I hadn't gone into the can for six games, I would have had a lot better chance to get 100 goals," he said.

But on March 17, he was back to being great again. As Oiler public relations man Bill Tuele would say, as he tried to keep track: "I think Gretzky has just set a record for setting records."

Gretzky even lost track. He forgot to collect the historic puck on one of them. With six games remaining in the regular season, his second goal of the game against the Pittsburgh Penguins broke Mike Bossy's NHL record of 85 for most goals in a season, including playoffs.

"I forgot all about it," said Wayne. "When it went on the public address system, the game had started again with the puck in play. I could have got it after the first whistle but I thought 'the heck with it.'"

Gretzky scored a hat-trick this night. It was his tenth of the season. It broke Bossy's record of nine. He passed his own record of 109 assists for the season with his 110th. Every time he scored, of course, it was a new single-season record, too.

Even Calgary caught cheering Edmonton star

A week later, in Calgary, Gretzky would reach another milestone. Against the Flames in game 76, he notched his 200th, 201st, 202nd and 203rd regular season points.

"I'll admit it," said his father, Walter. "Most of the things he's done I believed he'd do. All the other records I expected him to get. But this is something else. Two hundred points? No way! I'm like everybody else. I thought I'd never see the day."

While Walter was saying that, Wayne was denying it.

"It was my dad who first suggested the possibility to me," said Wayne. "Other than my father, I guess it was Gary Dornhoefer on a between-period interview in my first year in the league, on the night I scored six points in Toronto."

"The thing that boggled my mind the most, I guess," said Walter, "was getting the call from Wayne telling me and Phyllis to get on a plane and 'Come watch me get my 200th. You don't get a chance to see something like this every day.' It was like it didn't even cross my mind that he wouldn't get it tonight."

As he stood outside the Oiler dressing room, Walter Gretzky was surrounded by Calgary fans wanting HIS autograph. Dozens of them. One guy asked him to autograph the back of a $50 bill.

"I never thought I'd see the day," said Walter. "Me autographing the back of a $50 bill. That's a first."

But the story this night, due to the two cities involved, was that not only did nobody think they'd ever see the day that somebody would score 200 points in a single season of play in the NHL, nobody out West thought they'd ever see the day when a player wearing an Edmonton uniform would be given a standing ovation in Calgary.

"I've never seen it happen before, I guarantee you that," said Calgary sportscaster and sportswriter Eric Bishop, who had been watching sport in Calgary since he was in grade two in 1933.

Understand, of course, that the fans came to boo Gretzky. And they did so with lust.

"It's different here than anywhere else in the league," Wayne said. "I've been booed before but here they boo like they really mean it."

When the moment came, at 9:16 of the first period, seconds after Gretzky had fed team-mate Pat Hughes the usual perfect pass, there was a chorus of boos throughout the Calgary Corral. But then, one by one, it happened. The same people who were booing were suddenly hit by the thought that this was the history they'd come to watch. One by one, they started cheering. One by one, they started standing. Eventually everyone was on their feet making it memorable.

"It surprised me," Gretzky said. "I thought this was the last place this would ever happen to me. Because of the ovation they gave me, this means a little more than what happened in Buffalo when I broke Phil Esposito's record. It was a little more special tonight. I think it showed when a Canadian does something special, they'll drop everything to stand behind him and show their appreciation as fellow Canadians."

Gretzky's parents were stunned

both by the boos and the extent of the standing ovation.

"That's the worst I've ever heard Wayne booed," said Phyllis.

"But to follow those boos with the ovation for No. 200," said Walter, "well it reminds me again that booing is really quite the compliment and that booing doesn't mean much."

In the Oiler dressing room, Wayne was asking as many questions as he was answering.

"What's the record for shorthanded goals on one shift?" he asked. "If I hadn't hit a goal post, I'd have had three.

"I feel like the first guy to hit 100 points. Who was that anyway?"

It was Phil Esposito in 1968-69. And for the record, after four years in the league, Esposito and Gordie Howe still hadn't managed to get their 200th career point. Gretzky did it in a single season. His third.

Gretzky had two goals this night, numbers 89 and 90. And only four games remained. He needed 10 goals to get 100.

"I hope so," said Phyllis. "But I honestly don't think so."

"It's possible," said Wayne. "But I wouldn't bet on it unless it's with that guy's $50 bill he had my dad sign."

Accent shifts from Wayne to team

For the remainder of the season, the accent—from a record point of view— would not be on Gretzky but on the team.

When the club left Calgary and headed to Denver, the talk all day was which player would get what they called the "milestone marker." If the Oilers could score four goals against the Colorado Rockies, it would be their 400th goal of the season, and would break Boston Bruins' NHL record of 399.

"Bims," said Mark Messier. "A month ago we were all talking about it and we decided Bims (alias Bimbo, alias Garry Lariviere) should have the honor of scoring it. We had it planned. It would have been perfect. Bims would get his first goal as an Oiler and it would be no. 400 to break the record. But he screwed it up on us. He blew it for everybody when he went and scored by accident a couple of weeks early.

"If I had my choice now that Lariviere messed it up, I'd like it to be Kevin Lowe. I'd like him to get the goal because he's played so well all year and he's had the least recognition."

"My choice would be Lee Fogolin," said coach Glen Sather. "He was the first player we picked up in the merger draft. And he's our captain. That would be perfect. But whoever gets it tonight, I'd love it if it was somebody you wouldn't expect it to be. Everybody has played a part on this team, and it would be most appropriate if it was one of the unsung guys who got the big goal."

"I'd like it to be somebody like Cement," said Gretzky, of Dave Semenko. "The last while he's worked so hard to be viewed as a proven hockey player. It would be nice to see him get it."

"If I had my choice," said Dave Lumley, "there would be no choice. Gretz!"

"Who else?" said goaltender Ron Low. "He's got 90 percent of them. It would be fitting for him to get this record-breaker too."

"Gretzky," said Lee Fogolin. "He's done so much. He has every other record. For what he's meant to this team and for this accomplishment, because I'm sure we would never have hit 400 goals without him, it would be appropriate for him to get this one too. I mean, this is all just blowing me away. Last night, when the public address system announcer in Calgary said 'Scoring for Edmonton, number 99, Wayne Gretzky, his 90th goal of the season,' there was just something that hit everybody on the bench. We're used to everything and we almost expect it from him, But when the public address system announcer said 'his 90th goal of the season;' well, I looked at Kevin Lowe sitting beside me and he looked at me and at exactly the same second we both shook our heads and said 'unbelievable.'"

Gretzky scored points number 204, 205, and 206 this night and scored goal number 91. But he didn't get the "milestone marker."

It was Dave Lumley. And, in that it was Lumley who came close but got no cigar for his record run at the NHL consecutive game scoring streak, and in that it was Lumley's 30th of the season, everybody would agree, in the end, that it couldn't have been much more appropriate.

Besides, it was provided a double-barrelled trivia question: Who was the player who scored the last goal in the history of the World Hockey Association and set up the record 400th goal in the NHL?

Answer: Dave Semenko!

Semenko, who scored in the final playoff game in WHA history against the Winnipeg Jets, took the shot which set up the tap in for No. 400.

"It's nice to have done it in less than 78 games," said Lumley. "If we hadn't, the critics would have been out in full force saying we had more games to do it than the Bruins."

"I just wish I'd known that was No. 400," said Colorado netminder Chico Resch. "I'd have fought Lumley for the puck; then I could have traded it for a Gretzky stick. I don't have one of those and they're in such demand these days."

Leading the league in good times

When they hit Los Angeles, the final stop on the road trip, Gretzky and the Oilers had more records than a disc jockey. For months, every night in the dressing room of these amazing adolescents, there was nothing but platter chatter.

But the story wasn't just Wayne Gretzky, the team's success and the numbers. To tell the whole story of what had happened to the Oilers in 1981-82, you have to talk about the fun involved. And there was no better place to conduct a study on that subject than Los Angeles where it had become more than evident that quite likely no other team in pro sports was letting the good times roll quite like the Edmonton Oilers.

"I wouldn't trade this for anything," said Dave Lumley, who had his name placed in the NHL record books for the second time in two games when he scored a breakaway goal at 0:24 of the first period, ten seconds after Mark Messier had also scored on a breakaway. The Oilers thus beat, by five seconds yet, the record for the fastest two goals from the start of a game.

"We're the cockiest, most arrogant, fun-loving bunch of bananas in the league," said Lumley. "We're having the time of our lives."

"More than anything," said captain Lee Fogolin, "I think it's the fun which is making this team so successful. It's one of the big reasons we've got so good so fast. With the age of most of these guys and the zest they have for everything, on and off the ice, nobody has stopped to analyse ourselves. Everybody is just letting it happen and enjoying every minute of it. I've never seen a team which chirps and yells from the bench like this one. But it's not just that. It's everything."

Several Oilers' players attended a Hollywood party during the visit and found themselves in the company of such beautiful people as Morgan Fairchild, Hollywood's latest sex symbol, Priscilla Barnes of "Three's Company," and TV hosts Alan Thicke and Mike Douglas.

"I'm sitting in the penalty box tonight," said Lumley, who made several trips to that location, "and I couldn't keep my eyes off Morgan Fairchild. I'm sitting staring at her, paying no attention at all to the game. Half the guys on the bench are staring at her all night long and I'm thinking this is unreal. She's here because guys from our team got her tickets.

"The crazy thing is that we've got so many young guys, they probably think it's like this with every other team in the league."

Gretzky, of course, was the key to most of the doors which were opening for these Whiz Kids.

"It certainly wouldn't be like this without him," said Garry Lariviere, who said he made up his mind at this stop of how he was going to build his basement bar: "I'm going to have a picture taken with me and Wayne and I'm going to get it blown up bigger than lifesize and I'm going to put it right behind my bar and it'll dominate the room. I know when I retire that the big thing in my career will be not that I played in the NHL or for the Oilers, it'll be that I played with Wayne Gretzky."

Gretzky was to have appeared on the "The Tonight Show" with Johnny Carson earlier in the season, but was forced to cancel due to travel problems out of Quebec City. But he'd made his share of appearances including a spot on a Paul Anka spe-

cial. The Oilers had visited the set of M*A*S*H* as a team, and they had more Hollywood types hanging around them on their visits here than hung around the Los Angeles Kings.

"This is unreal," said Messier, who scored his 47th and 48th goals of the year (he'd get No. 50 before the schedule ended) in a 6-2 win over the team the Oilers would meet in the Stanley Cup playoffs.

The Oilers, who finished the season with a 3-1 win over Winnipeg at home, ended up in second place overall with 111 points—37 points more and 12 places ahead of where they were the year before.

But the fun was about to end for the happy-go-lucky players of the Edmonton Oilers. Suddenly their lifestyle was about to change. And they wouldn't handle it well.

Whiz Kids become Was Kids

It was a strange space the Oilers sat in as they contemplated their third Stanley Cup playoff experience.

Call it a change of life.

It could never be the same for them.

But did they realize that?

Yesterday, as in twenty-four hours earlier, they were the Whiz Kids of 1981-82. They'd become Canada's Team. Yesterday they were the team which had upset the Montreal Canadiens in three straight Stanley Cup playoff games and given the New York Islanders their toughest test enroute to a second straight Cup title. Yesterday they were the Scoro Squad, the club which hit 111 points in the standings and ended up with 417 goals.

Now they were required to play a different role. Today they began to be the hunted instead of the hunters. Today, instead of throwing out their

"Fantasy Island" quotes, they have to talk about not being overconfident, about having to take a 17th place team in the NHL seriously in the playoffs and all that other boring, but oh-so-true stuff. Today, their age of innocence would be over.

"It's going to be strange," said assistant coach Harris on the eve of the series with Los Angeles. "Last year we beat the Montreal Canadiens. This year we finished ahead of them in the standings. In a way we've kind of become the Montreal Canadiens.

"The difference is that it hasn't sunk in. If somebody told us in September that we'd finish second overall and end up with 111 points in the standings well, we figured somewhere between 9th and 12th overall. This team has played beyond anybody's expectations since the middle of last March. Instead of getting a little better year by year, we did it all at once. Now strange thoughts cross your mind. Like could the bubble burst? Maybe we might not be as strong a team next year. Maybe, because of circumstances in our future, we might never have a season like this again."

Maybe, indeed.

The Whiz Kids put themselves in instant danger of becoming the Was Kids in game one. They blew a 4-1 lead as the Kings came from behind to beat the Oilers at home 10-8.

"Maybe it was nervousness," said Sather. "Panic seemed to set in. You could see it. All of a sudden the puck was a hot potato. Our entire game fell apart. We made dreadful mistakes. The only game I think we played worse was against Buffalo in the preseason, we were horrible.

"We find out right now, in one heck of a hurry, if we really are legitimate Stanley Cup contenders. It's our first test on the Stanley Cup trail. We might as well find out about ourselves right off the bat."

In game two, the Oilers were still rattled.

Mark Messier, for example, the young man who only a few days earlier was skating past the bench in Los Angeles laughing, fainted in the walkway between the dressing room and the bench.

They'd panicked again.

But they won. Gretzky scored in overtime.

"With some guys, I'd have bailed out," said Lumley, about his part in the screened shot for the winner. "But not with Wayne. When he's shooting, you know he's going to hit the net, so I stood there."

In game three, the Oilers choked. Fans back in Edmonton were asking how it was even possible. How could any self-respecting team allow it to happen. How do you gas a 5-0 lead?

"Stupid hockey," said Gretzky.

"It could only happen to us, the way we played so stupid in this series. Wasn't it bad enough we had to kill so many penalties without being stupid enough to take even more in the third period? Were we stupid enough to think it wouldn't catch up? It did!" commented coach Sather.

"This time it wasn't so much panic as playing stupid," said Gretzky, who was given an obscene "Gretzky sucks" chant by more than half the crowd when he skated away from a free-for-all wrestling match at the boards.

"This series should be over. We've blown a 4-1 lead and now a 5-0 lead. Now there are five or six of us who are one game away from having to go the Europe for the world championships instead of being two series away from the Stanley Cup final. I want this cup — the Stanley Cup — not the one they play for in Europe."

Gretzky called 'Cry Baby' by Kings

If by now Wayne Gretzky figured he'd witnessed every possible reaction to him, he was in for a surprise in game four of the series.

Thousands of fans, reacting to "cry baby" quotes supplied by the King players, took hankies out of their pockets and waved them tauntingly at Gretzky whenever he was on the ice.

The Kings pointed to an incident where Dave Lumley found himself in the middle of a skirmish in game three and everyone rushed to the scene except Gretzky who instead skated to centre ice.

"He's just a player who likes to score goals," said Kings' Jay Wells, "but I consider him one of the worst team men in the league."

"He's a great hockey player but he's a bit of a cry baby," said Kings' coach Don Perry.

The Oilers rushed to the defence of Gretzky in the controversy.

"Gretzky is the best team man I've ever played alongside," said captain Lee Fogolin. "He's the greatest player in the game, yet he's the most humble player in our dressing room. He's always trying to give somebody else credit or to help somebody else score a goal when he needs one, like Mark Messier when he was going for his 50th, and Dave Lumley when he had his consecutive game scoring streak going."

"What does he want Wayne to do?" said Lumley, "punch a guy in the face and break his hand?"

"There's no sense in me getting thrown out of the game," said Gretzky. "The Kings would love to get me in a situation like that. I'll do my talking on the ice and let everybody else do their talking in the papers.

The biggest thing all that stuff did was take the crowd away from their hockey club and give it to me. They were all booing me instead of cheering for their team. I don't mind that at all."

Gretzky and the Oilers felt that was a major factor in the Oilers winning the game four, 3 to 2.

But if Gretzky was the centre of attention in Los Angeles, he was AWOL in the fifth and deciding game of the series back in-Edmonton the next night. His play was highly reminiscent of the final game of the Canada Cup at the beginning of the season.

There were dozens of reasons why the Oilers, who turned from wonders in the regular season to weak-kneed wimps in the playoffs, didn't win the series. Inconsistent goaltending. Penalties and giveaways. Panic and stupidity. There were a dozen Oilers who messed up in the playoffs, but because of his stature most fans would eventually forget the team's failures and would even forget Gretzky's overtime goal in game two and his generally great play in the first four games and choose to remember only that The Great Gretzky was invisible in the final game.

"This was worse," said Gretzky, comparing what happened to him against the Kings to what had happened to him against the Russians in the Canada Cup.

A tired Gretzky shipped to Finland

He played in seven Canada Cup games, then six exhibition games for the Oilers, and 80 regular season league games, the all-star game, and five games in the playoffs.

When Gretzky returned, along with team-mate Kevin Lowe, to his apartment after the loss to Los Angeles, he received a phone call from Alan Eagleson inviting both himself and Lowe to join Team Canada at the World Championships in Finland as last-minute additions.

For the most part Gretzky did not play well in Europe. His fabulous season in the end, it would be written, had been framed by failures.

When he returned home he had plenty to analyze — the Oilers' failure in the playoffs and the Team Canada failures against the Soviets at the beginning and the end of the season.

"I guess one of the things I'm going to remember most was after the second game against the Soviets," said Wayne. "Kevin and I couldn't get to sleep. We stayed up all night.

"Kevin is a good fundamentalist and analyst of hockey. He's going to be a coach some day. But I've got my own ideas too. We sat in our hotel room for four or five hours, until 4 or 5 A.M., arguing. He had his reasons why we got beat again, and I had mine. When we finally turned out the lights and went to bed, we hadn't settled anything.

"I guess my argument was politics. And Kevin's was hockey. I'm going over to visit the Soviet Union this summer and old-time Russian coach Anatoly Tarasov has invited me to attend a couple of Red Army practices as his guest. It's amazing. On June 27, the Russian hockey team is going to be right back at it, practicing. Are they crazy? My argument is how can we beat that? Their players have no choice. Nine out of ten of our players would say 'no way.' They have 300 million people and we have 25 million. They should be better.

"Kevin argued that we should have

the discipline to work just as hard. He says we can do it if we want to do it. I say it's impossible in our system. He says it's not. We just sat up and argued, like a couple of hockey fans, for hours.

"Until that night after the Soviet game, we talked mostly about the Oilers and how impossible it seemed that teams like Vancouver, Los Angeles, and Chicago, who had so many problems all season, were still alive in the Stanley Cup playoffs while we weren't.

"I know how Kevin and I feel. We didn't have any argument there. I just hope everybody on our club feels the same way.

"We realize now that our team needs some changes. I think Glen Sather knows that too. There are lessons to be learned and we have to learn them. I'm not pointing any fingers, because we win as a team and we lose as a team, but if we're going to get better then a lot of our people had better get straightened out. I guess we got carried away with who we thought we were and we proved that we can't just throw the sticks out on the ice and expect to win.

"You can analyse upside down and inside out, like we did the first few days in our room over in Finland, and what it all comes down to is maturity. If we don't learn our lesson there, if we don't come back next year as a more mature hockey team, the same thing is going to happen to us again."

Gretzky admitted he didn't prove much at the World Championships.

"I accept the roses when they are thrown when I play well, and I have to accept the criticism when I don't," he said in response to the suggestion that he now had a valid knock on him after he did not play well in the 8-1 loss to the Soviets in the final of the

Canada Cup, the final game of the series against Los Angeles in the playoffs, and in the two key games against the Russians at the World Championships.

"We should have won the first game with the Soviets in the World Championships. We had three situations and didn't score on any of them. That was the turning point. Then I lost that crucial face-off in the second game against the Soviets and that cost us the hockey game.

"I guess if I proved anything over there, I proved it in the last game against Sweden," he said of his three-goal two-assist game.

"For everybody who was saying I was exhausted, tired, and worn down, I think I proved something by playing the best game I played all year — I honestly feel that was the best game I played all year — in the last game I played.

"What happened has given me a challenge for the future. Whether you're playing for the Edmonton Oilers, Team Canada, or if you're playing street hockey, you're playing for a team and you're playing to win. I had a good season, but in the end, because of the way everything turned out, it didn't mean much.

"I know now that I won't be satisfied with much until I have a Stanley Cup ring on my finger."

Gretzky and Tretiak meet on Soviet soil

Although the Soviets did their level best on the ice to spoil Gretzky's greatest season, they certainly made up for it in the summer. Wayne and his entire family were guests of the Russians in Moscow and it was an experience of a lifetime.

When they said goodbye to Vladislav Tretiak at the Moscow airport, the kids cried.

"Brent was really in tears," said Walter Gretzky of his youngest son. "And Glenn was crying too. We all became very close to Tretiak and his wife."

What was it like? "Let's put it this way," said Walter. "I wouldn't want to live there. But for Wayne and the kids it was a wonderful experience they'll remember for the rest of their lives.

"What they'll remember most," Walter said, "is the Tretiaks and a group of hockey-playing kids in Moscow.

"Tretiak's wife was wonderful. She stayed up all night — didn't sleep a wink — the night before Wayne, Vicki, and the boys were to visit. The whole family, a whole entourage of twelve people, were invited. But we were told it was a very small apartment so Wayne and Vicki and the boys went but the rest of us didn't go. Mrs. Tretiak was so nervous about the visit. I guess she was running around before Wayne got there, straightening pictures on the wall and stuff like that. Just like we'd be if they came to our house.

"Tretiak is a very nice man and the kids just adored him. The kids had a chance to go in on the net and take shots at him. How many kids in Canada can say they took shots on Vladislav Tretiak? Brent even scored. He came back to where I was standing and said, 'Dad, did you see that?' He was especially tickled when there was a thing for the film we were doing where Tretiak jumped on top of Brent. Not hard so he hurt him. Just like a father playing with his son. It was beautiful. I think that's what Brent will remember most.

"One of the things I'll remember most were the Soviet kids themselves. They are just like our kids. Their equipment and skates aren't nearly as good as the stuff our kids wear, but they're the same kids. There were always one or two of them fooling around. They were very friendly to our kids."

The things Walter will remember best about his most famous son involve the public appearances with Tretiak.

"They were pictured together on the front page of the newspaper. I think it was the front, they only have two pages in their newspaper. They signed autographs together at the Kremlin. I couldn't believe how much Tretiak enjoyed signing autographs. The people knew who Wayne was. Some of the people would go to Wayne to get his autograph first. And others would go to Tretiak to get his autograph. There's no question that Tretiak is very well known over there. And boy, is his wife proud of him.

"Tretiak came to us after Wayne and the kids visited his apartment and gave everybody, all twelve of us, a gift. He didn't want anybody to feel left out at all.

"Wayne thought he had an impressive collection of trophies and things, but Tretiak had a collection of medals that Wayne just couldn't believe. We went to the famous circus on ice and that was a big thrill. They introduced Wayne and Tretiak in the crowd and I couldn't believe the response. I expected them to applaud politely. They cheered and cheered. It was really noisy. It was something that I'm sure Wayne will remember probably better than anything, from this.

"Heck, I'm sure Wayne will remember every moment. After all, who else has it ever happened to?"

Exactly.

Who else has *all of this* ever happened to? The records. The Rocket's. Espo's. Orr's. The awards. Twenty-one years old and three straight Hart Trophies as the Most Valuable Player in the NHL, the last one by unanimous selection. The Great Gretzky. Twenty-one years old, and he'd become The Greatest.

Bobby Hull, in presenting Gretzky with the Art Ross Trophy, for his 92 goals and 212 points, was left to sum it up.

"He's had the greatest impact I've ever seen in any sport," said Hull.

"Wayne has done more for the game of hockey than any other person who has ever played or likely ever will."

The Statistical Record

GRETZKY, WAYNE (GRETZ-kee)
Born, Brantford, Ont., January 26, 1961.
Center. Shoots left. 5' 11", 165 lbs.
Last amateur club: Sault Ste. Marie Greyhounds (Jrs.)

Season	Club	Lea	Regular Schedule					Playoffs				
			GP	G	A	TP	PIM	GP	G	A	TP	PIM
1978-79	Indianapolis	WHA	8	3	3	6	0	....	....	....	....	....
1978-79	Edmonton	WHA	72	43	61	104	19	13	*10	10	*20	2
1979-80abc	Edmonton	NHL	79	51	*86	*137	21	3	2	1	3	0
1980-81ade fg	Edmonton	NHL	80	55	*109	*164	28	9	7	14	21	4
1981-82ade fgi	Edmonton	NHL	80	*92	*120	*212	26	5	5	7	12	8
	NHL Totals		239	198	315	513	75	17	12	22	36	12
	WHA Totals		80	46	64	110	19	13	10	10	20	2

*Establishes new record.

A. Won Hart Trophy.
B. Won Lady Byng Trophy.
C. Second All-Star Team (center).
D. First All-Star Team (center).
E. Won Art Ross Trophy.
F. NHL record for assists in regular season.
G. NHL record for points in regular season.
I. Won Lester B. Pearson Trophy.

Reclaimed by Edmonton as an under-age junior prior to Expansion Draft, June 9, 1979.
Claimed as priority selection by Edmonton, June 9, 1979.

Most Assists, One Season:
120 — Wayne Gretzky, Edmonton Oilers, 1981-82. (80 games)
109 — Wayne Gretzky, Edmonton Oilers, 1980-81. (80 games)
102 — Bobby Orr, Boston Bruins, 1970-71. (78 games)
90 — Bobby Orr, Boston Bruins, 1978-79. (79 games)

Most Points, One Season:
212 — Wayne Gretzky, Edmonton Oilers, 1981-82. (80 games)
164 — Wayne Gretzky, Edmonton Oilers, 1980-81. (80 games)
152 — Phil Esposito, Boston Bruins, 1970-71. (78 games)
147 — Mike Bossy, New York Islanders, 1981-82. (80 games)
145 — Phil Esposito, Boston Bruins, 1973-74. (78 games)

Highest Assist-Per-Game Average, One Season (Among Players With 35-Or-More Assists):
1.50 — Wayne Gretzky, Edmonton Oilers, 1981-82, with 120 assists in 80 games.
1.36 — Wayne Gretzky, Edmonton Oilers, 1980-81, with 109 assists in 80 games.
1.31 — Bobby Orr, Boston Bruins, 1970-71, with 102 assists in 78 games.

1.22 — Bobby Orr, Boston Bruins, 1973-74, with 90 assists in 74 games.
1.17 — Bobby Clarke, Philadelphia Flyers, 1975-76, with 89 assists in 76 games.

Highest Points-Per-Game Average, One Season (Among Players With 50-Or-More Points):
2.65 — Wayne Gretzky, Edmonton Oilers, 1981-82, with 212 points in 80 games.
2.05 — Wayne Gretzky, Edmonton Oilers, 1980-81, with 164 points in 80 games
1.97 — Bill Cowley, Boston Bruins, 1943-44, with 71 points in 36 games.
1.95 — Phil Esposito, Boston Bruins, 1970-71, with 152 points in 78 games.

Most Assists, One Season, Including Playoffs:
127 — Wayne Gretzky, Edmonton Oilers, 1981-82, 120 assists in 80 regular-season games and 7 assists in 5 playoff games.
123 — Wayne Gretzky, Edmonton Oilers, 1980-81, 109 assists in 80 regular-season games and 14 assists in 9 playoff games.
109 — Bobby Orr, Boston Bruins, 1970-71, 102 assists in 78 regular-season games and 7 assists in 7 playoff games.
104 — Bobby Orr, Boston Bruins, 1973-74, 90

assists in 74 regular-season games and 14 assists in 16 playoff games.

Most Points, One Season, Including Playoffs:

224 — **Wayne Gretzky**, Edmonton Oilers, 1981-82, 212 points in 80 regular-season games and 12 points in 5 playoff games.

185 — **Wayne Gretzky**, Edmonton Oilers, 1980-81, 164 points in 80 regular-season games and 21 points in 9 playoff games.

174 — Mike Bossy, New York Islanders, 1981-82, 147 points in 80 regular-season games and 27 points in 19 playoff games.

162 — Phil Esposito, Boston Bruins, 1970-71, 152 points in 78 regular-season games and 10 points in 7 playoff games.

— Guy Lafleur, Montreal Canadiens, 1976-77, 136 points in 80 regular-season games and 26 points in 14 playoff games.

159 — Phil Esposito, Boston Bruins, 1973-74, 145 points in 78 regular-season games and 14 points in 16 playoff games.

Most Goals By A Player In His First NHL Season (Non-Rookie):

51 — **Wayne Gretzky**, Edmonton Oilers, 1979-80. (80 games)

46 — Blair MacDonald, Edmonton Oilers, 1979-80. (80 games)

44 — Mike Rogers, Hartford Whalers, 1979-80. (80 games)

Most Assists, One Season, By A Center:

120 — **Wayne Gretzky**, Edmonton Oilers, 1981-82. (80 games)

109 — **Wayne Gretzky**, Edmonton Oilers, 1980-81. (80 games)

93 — Peter Stastny, Quebec Nordiques, 1981-82. (80 games)

89 — Bobby Clarke, Philadelphia Flyers, 1974-75, 1975-76. (80 games)

87 — Bryan Trottier, New York Islanders, 1978-79. (80 games)

Most Assists By A Player In His First NHL Season (Non-Rookie):

86 — **Wayne Gretzky**, Edmonton Oilers, 1979-80. (80 games)

61 — Mike Rogers, Hartford Whalers, 1979-80. (80 games)

56 — Mark Howe, Hartford Whalers, 1979-80. (80 games)

Most Points, One Season, By A Center:

212 — **Wayne Gretzky**, Edmonton Oilers, 1981-82. (80 games)

164 — **Wayne Gretzky**, Edmonton Oilers, 1980-81. (80 games)

152 — Phil Esposito, Boston Bruins, 1970-71. (78 games)

145 — Phil Esposito, Boston Bruins, 1973-74. (78 games)

Most Points By A Player In His First NHL Season (Non-Rookie):

137 — **Wayne Gretzky**, Edmonton Oilers, 1979-80. (80 games)

105 — Mike Rogers, Hartford Whalers, 1979-80. (80 games)

94 — Blair MacDonald, Edmonton Oilers, 1979-80. (80 games)

Most Assists, One Game:

7 — **Billy Taylor**, Detroit Red Wings, March 16, 1947, at Chicago. Detroit 10, Chicago 6.

— **Wayne Gretzky**, Edmonton Oilers, Feb. 15, 1980, at Edmonton. Edmonton 8, Washington 2.

Most Assists, One Game, By A Player In His First NHL Season:

7 — **Wayne Gretzky**, Edmonton Oilers, Feb. 15, 1980, at Edmonton. Edmonton 8, Washington 2.

5 — Jim McFadden, Detroit Red Wings, Nov. 23, 1947, at Chicago. Detroit 9, Chicago 3.

— Mark Howe, Hartford Whalers, Jan. 30, 1980, at Hartford. Hartford 8, Boston 2.

— Anton Stastny, Quebec Nordiques, Feb. 22, 1981, at Washington. Quebec 11, Washington 7.

Most Goals, One Period:

4 — Harvey (Busher) Jackson, Toronto Maple Leafs, Nov. 20, 1934, at St. Louis, third period. Toronto 5, St. Louis Eagles 2.

— Max Bentley, Chicago Black Hawks, Jan. 28, 1943, at Chicago, third period. Chicago 10, New York Rangers 1.

— Clint Smith, Chicago Black Hawks, March 4, 1945, at Chicago, third period. Chicago 6, Montreal Canadiens 4.

— Red Berenson, St. Louis Blues, Nov. 7, 1968, at Philadelphia, second period. St. Louis 8, Philadelphia Flyers 0.

— **Wayne Gretzky**, Edmonton Oilers, Feb. 18, 1981, at Edmonton, third period. Edmonton 9, St. Louis 2

Longest Consecutive Assist-Scoring Streak:

14 Games — **Wayne Gretzky**, Edmonton Oilers, 1981-82. 26 assists during streak.

— Bobby Orr, Boston Bruins, 1970-71. 23 assists during streak.

— Jude Drouin, Minnesota Notrh Stars, 1971-72. 21 assists during streak.

— Stan Mikita, Chicago Black Hawks, 1967-68. 18 assists during streak.

Longest Consecutive Point-Scoring Streak:

18 Games — Guy Lafleur, Montreal Canadiens, 1976-77. 19 goals, 42 assists, 61 points during streak.

15 Games — Bryan Trottier, New Yrok Islanders, 1981-82. 28 goals, 27 assists, 55 points during streak.

14 Games — Wayne Gretzky, Edmonton Oilers, 1981-82. 28 goals, 38 assists, 66 points during streak.

Most Points, One Game, By A Player In His First NHL Season:

8 — Peter Stastny, Quebec Nordiques, Feb. 22, 1981, at Washington. 4 goals, 4 assists. Quebec 11, Washington 7.
Anton Stastny, Quebec Nordiques, Feb 22, 1981, at Washington. 3 goals, 5 assists. Quebec 11, Washington 7.

7 — Wayne Gretzky, Edmonton Oilers, Feb. 15, 1980, at Edmonton. 7 assists. Edmonton 8, Washington 2.

6 — Wayne Gretzky, Edmonton Oilers, March 29, 1980, at Toronto. 2 goals, 4 assists. Edmonton 8, Toronto 5.

Highest Assist-Per-Game Average, Career (Among Players With 300 Or More Assists):

1.318 — Wayne Gretkzy, Edmonton Oilers, 315 assists, 239 games from 1979-80 through 1981-82.

.982 — Bobby Orr, Boston Bruins, Chicago Black Hawks, 645 assists, 657 games from 1966-67 through 1978-79.

.893 — Bryan Trottier, New York Islanders, 482 assists, 540 games from 1975-76 through 1981-82.

.807 — Marcel Dionne, Detroit, Los Angeles, 692 assists, 857 games from 1971-72 through 1981-82.

Highest Points-Per-Game Average, Career (Among Players With 500 Or More Points):

2.146 — Wayne Gretzky, Edmonton Oilers, 513 points (198 goals, 315 assists), 239 games from 1979-80 through 1981-82.

1.486 — Mike Bossy, New York Islnders, 575 points (305 goals, 270 assists), 387 games from 1977-78 through 1981-82.

1.407 — Bryan Trottier, New York Islanders, 760 points (278 goals, 482 assists), 540 games from 1975-76 through 1981-82.

1.393 — Bobby Orr, Boston Bruins, Chicago Black Hawks, 915 points (270 goals, 645 assists), 657 games from 1966-67 through 1978-79.

NHL Points-Per-Game Leaders, One Season (Among players with 50 points or more in one season)

Player	Team	Season	Games	Points	Average
Wayne Gretzky	Edmonton Oilers	1981-82	80	212	2.65
Wayne Gretzky	Edmonton Oilers	1980-81	80	164	2.05
Bill Cowley	Boston Bruins	1943-44	36	71	1.97
Phil Esposito	Boston Bruins	1970-71	78	152	1.95
Phil Esposito	Boston Bruins	1973-74	78	145	1.86
Mike Bossy	New York Islanders	1981-82	80	147	1.84
Bobby Orr	Boston Bruins	1970-71	78	139	1.78
Bryan Trottier	New York Islanders	1978-79	76	134	1.76
Phil Esposito	Boston Bruins	1971-72	76	133	1.75
Peter Stastny	Quebec Nordiques	1981-82	80	139	1.74
Wayne Gretzky	Edmonton Oilers	1979-80	79	137	1.73

NHL Assists-Per-Game Leaders, One Season (Among players with 35 assists or more in one season)

Player	Team	Season	Games	Assists	Average
Wayne Gretzky	Edmonton Oilers	1981-82	80	120	1.50
Wayne Gretzky	Edmonton Oilers	1980-81	80	109	1.36
Bobby Orr	Boston Bruins	1970-71	78	102	1.31
Bobby Orr	Boston Bruins	1973-74	74	90	1.22
Bobby Clarke	Philadelphia Flyers	1975-76	76	89	1.17
Peter Stastny	Quebec Nordiques	1981-82	80	93	1.16
Bobby Orr	Boston Bruins	1969-70	76	87	1.15
Bryan Trottier	New York Islanders	1978-79	76	87	1.14
Bobby Orr	Boston Bruins	1972-73	63	72	1.14
Bill Cowley	Boston Bruins	1943-44	36	41	1.14
Bobby Clarke	Philadelphia Flyers	1974-75	80	89	1.11
Bobby Orr	Boston Bruins	1974-75	80	89	1.11
Wayne Gretzky	Edmonton Oilers	1979-80	79	86	1.09
Denis Savard	Chicago Black Hawks	1981-82	80	87	1.09

Gretzky vs NHL Opposition: Bruins, Buffalo do the best job

	W	L	T	1979-80				1980-81				1981-82				Totals			
				GP	G	A	Pts	GP	G	A	Pts	GP	G	A	Pts	GP	G	A	Pts
LA	7	4	5	4	6	6	12	4	5	4	9	8	13	9	22	16	24	19	43
Cal	7	6	3	4	3	3	6	4	3	5	8	8	9	11	20	16	15	19	34
Pitt	8	2	1	4	7	5	12	4	2	7	9	3	5	5	10	11	14	17	31
Van	8	6	2	4	2	1	3	4	2	7	9	8	4	14	18	16	8	22	30
St.L	4	4	2	3	2	4	6	4	6	7	13	3	6	4	10	10	14	15	29
Tor	6	3	2	4	4	10	14	4	4	5	9	3	4	1	5	11	12	16	28
Chi	7	3	1	4	0	5	5	4	4	8	12	3	4	7	11	11	8	20	28
NYI	4	5	1	4	5	6	11	4	4	3	7	3	2	7	9	11	11	16	27
Phil	4	6	1	4	1	5	6	4	6	2	8	3	9	3	12	11	16	10	26
Que	4	7	0	4	3	4	7	4	4	6	10	3	4	5	9	11	11	15	26
Wash	6	3	2	4	2	9	11	4	2	4	6	3	4	5	9	11	8	18	26
Wpg	8	2	1	4	4	2	6	4	4	9	13	3	2	4	6	11	10	15	25
Det	5	3	3	4	3	5	8	4	1	7	8	3	2	7	9	11	6	19	25
Col	7	7	1	4	2	4	6	4	0	6	6	7	4	8	12	15	6	18	24
Minn	4	3	4	4	2	2	4	4	1	5	6	3	5	7	12	11	8	14	22
Hart	5	3	3	4	1	2	3	4	2	8	10	3	5	3	8	11	8	13	21
Mtl	3	6	2	4	3	3	6	4	1	6	7	3	1	6	7	11	5	15	20
NYR	5	5	1	4	0	2	2	4	3	5	8	3	4	5	9	11	7	12	19
Buff	4	4	4	4	1	6	7	4	0	2	2	3	4	2	6	11	5	10	15
Bos	1	8	2	4	0	2	2	4	1	3	4	3	1	4	5	11	2	9	11

As Gretzky Goes: So go the Edmonton Oilers

	1979-80				1980-81				1981-82				NHL Totals			
	G	W	L	T	G	W	L	T	G	W	L	T	G	W	L	T
0 points	17	1	15	1	13	0	9	4	8	1	6	1	38	2	30	6
1 point	21	3	11	7	23	6	12	5	11	5	4	2	55	14	27	14
2 points	22	13	6	3	16	3	10	3	22	10	5	7	60	26	21	13
3 points	10	4	5	1	13	8	3	2	16	11	1	4	39	23	9	7
4 points	6	4	1	1	8	6	1	1	9	7	1	1	23	17	3	3
5 points	1	1	0	0	5	4	0	1	12	12	0	0	18	17	0	1
6 points	1	1	0	0	1	1	0	0	1	1	0	0	3	3	0	0
7 points	1	1	0	0	1	1	0	0	1	1	0	0	3	3	0	0
3 or more	19	11	6	2	28	20	4	4	39	32	2	4	86	63	12	10

Gretzky By Month: He likes the 'New Year'

	1979-80				1980-81				1981-82				NHL Totals			
	GP	G	A	Pts	GP	G	A	Pts	GP	G	A	Pts	GP	G	A	Pts
Oct	9	2	8	10	9	5	11	16	13	13	14	27	31	20	33	53
Nov	13	8	17	25	14	6	17	23	13	18	19	37	40	32	53	85
Dec	12	9	9	18	12	6	11	17	14	19	25	44	38	34	45	79
Jan	15	9	16	25	14	10	25	35	15	17	21	38	44	36	62	98
Feb	14	7	18	25	14	15	15	30	11	15	20	35	39	37	53	90
Mar	13	14	16	30	14	11	23	34	13	10	20	30	40	35	59	94
Apr	3	2	2	4	3	2	7	9	1	0	1	1	7	4	10	14

Gretzky By Ten Game Blocks
Second half, better than the first

Game	1979-80				1980-81				1981-82				NHL Totals			
	GP	G	A	Pts	GP	G	A	Pts	GP	G	A	Pts	GP	G	A	Pts
1-10	9	2	8	10	10	5	11	16	10	7	10	17	29	14	29	43
11-20	10	7	12	19	10	4	11	15	10	14	13	27	30	25	36	61
21-30	10	6	10	16	10	4	12	16	10	10	20	30	30	20	42	62
31-40	10	7	6	13	10	8	15	23	10	19	15	34	30	34	36	70
41-50	10	6	14	20	10	6	17	23	10	11	14	25	30	23	45	68
51-60	10	7	14	21	10	12	9	21	10	9	14	23	30	28	37	65
61-70	10	6	10	16	10	11	10	21	10	12	19	31	30	29	39	68
71-80	10	10	12	22	10	5	24	29	10	10	15	25	30	25	51	76
First half	39	22	36	58	40	21	49	70	40	50	58	108	119	93	143	236
Second half	40	29	50	79	40	34	60	94	40	42	62	104	120	105	206	311

Gretzky Home and Away
Better balance than most

	1979-80				1980-81				1981-82				NHL Totals			
	GP	G	A	Pts	GP	G	A	Pts	GP	G	A	Pts	GP	G	A	Pts
Home	40	28	49	77	40	29	62	91	40	59	65	124	120	116	176	292
Away	39	23	37	60	40	26	47	73	40	33	55	88	119	82	139	221

Gretzky Game By Game Statistics

Eighteen, Going On Nineteen
Tied for Tops (1979-80) for Openers

No.	Date	H/A	Team	Scr	W/L	Game Totals			1979-80 Totals			N.H.L. Career			Majors (Incl. WHA)		
						G	A	Pts	G	A	Pts	G	A	Pts	G	A	Pts
1	Oct 10	A	Chi	4-2	L	0	1	1	0	1	1	0	1	1	46	65	111
2	Oct 13	H	Det	3-3	T	0	1	1	0	2	2	0	2	2	46	66	112
3	Oct 14	H	Van	4-4	T	1	1	2	1	3	4	1	3	4	47	67	114
4	Oct 19	H	Que	6-3	W	0	3	3	1	6	7	1	6	7	47	70	117
5	Oct 21	H	Minn	5-5	T	1	1	2	2	7	9	2	7	9	48	71	119
6	Oct 23	A	NYI	3-3	T	0	1	1	2	8	10	2	8	10	48	72	120
7	Oct 24	A	NYR	10-2	L	0	0	0	2	8	10	2	8	10	48	72	120
8	Oct 26	A	Atl	7-3	L	0	0	0	2	8	10	2	8	10	48	72	120
9	Oct 28	H	Wash	6-4	L	0	0	0	2	8	10	2	8	10	48	72	120
10	Oct 30	A	StL	2-1	L	- - - - -Did not play, injured -											

Eighteen, Going On Nineteen
Tied for Tops (1979-80) for Openers

No.	Date	H/A	Team	Scr	W/L	Game Totals G	A	Pts	1979-80 Totals G	A	Pts	N.H.L. Career G	A	Pts	Majors (Incl. WHA) G	A	Pts
11	Nov 2	H	NYI	7-5	W	2	1	3	4	9	13	4	9	13	50	73	123
12	Nov 4	H	Bos	2-1	L	0	1	1	4	10	14	4	10	14	50	74	124
13	Nov 7	A	Det	5-3	L	1	1	2	5	11	16	5	11	16	51	75	126
14	Nov 8	A	Bos	4-2	L	0	0	0	5	11	16	5	11	16	51	75	126
15	Nov 11	H	Tor	6-3	L	0	2	2	5	13	18	5	13	18	51	77	128
16	Nov 13	A	Wash	5-3	W	1	1	2	6	14	20	6	14	20	52	78	130
17	Nov 15	A	Phil	5-3	L	0	2	2	6	16	22	6	16	22	52	80	132
18	Nov 17	A	Hart	4-0	L	0	0	0	6	16	22	6	16	22	52	80	132
19	Nov 18	A	Buff	9-7	L	1	2	3	7	18	25	7	18	25	53	82	135
20	Nov 21	A	Tor	4-4	T	2	2	4	9	20	29	9	20	29	55	84	139
21	Nov 24	H	Phil	2-2	T	0	1	1	9	21	30	9	21	30	55	85	140
22	Nov 28	H	Chi	4-2	W	0	2	2	9	23	32	9	23	32	55	87	142
23	Nov 30	H	NYI	5-3	W	1	2	3	10	25	35	10	25	35	56	89	145
24	Dec 5	A	Minn	6-1	L	0	0	0	10	25	35	10	25	35	56	89	145
25	Dec 7	A	Wpg	8-3	L	0	0	0	10	25	35	10	25	35	56	89	145
26	Dec 9	H	Hart	3-0	W	1	1	2	11	26	37	11	26	37	57	90	147
27	Dec 12	H	Atl	5-5	T	0	1	1	11	27	38	11	27	38	57	91	148
28	Dec 14	H	Mtl	5-3	W	1	1	2	12	28	40	12	28	40	58	92	150
29	Dec 16	H	Wpg	4-3	L	1	1	2	13	29	42	13	29	42	59	93	152
30	Dec 19	H	Det	6-4	L	2	1	3	15	30	45	15	30	45	61	94	155
31	Dec 21	A	Col	5-4	L	0	1	1	15	31	46	15	31	46	61	95	156
32	Dec 22	A	LA	9-3	L	2	1	3	17	32	49	17	32	49	63	96	159
33	Dec 26	H	Col	4-3	W	1	1	2	18	33	51	18	33	51	64	97	161
34	Dec 28	A	Van	5-3	W	1	0	1	19	33	52	19	33	52	65	97	162
35	Dec 30	H	Que	2-1	L	0	1	1	19	34	53	19	34	53	65	98	163
36	Jan 2	H	Hart	3-3	T	0	1	1	19	35	54	19	35	54	65	99	164
37	Jan 5	H	LA	3-3	T	2	0	2	21	35	56	21	35	56	67	99	166
38	Jan 7	H	Mtl	4-3	L	0	0	0	21	35	56	21	35	56	67	99	166
39	Jan 9	A	Que	6-2	L	1	0	1	22	35	57	22	35	57	68	99	167
40	Jan 11	H	NYR	6-2	L	0	1	1	22	36	58	22	36	58	68	100	168
41	Jan 13	H	Buff	6-5	W	0	2	2	22	38	60	22	38	60	68	102	170
42	Jan 16	A	Wash	5-2	W	1	1	2	23	39	62	23	39	62	69	103	172
43	Jan 17	A	Bos	7-1	L	0	0	0	23	39	62	23	39	62	69	103	172
44	Jan 19	A	Pitt	5-2	W	2	2	4	25	41	66	25	41	66	71	105	176
45	Jan 20	A	Buff	4-4	T	0	1	1	25	42	67	25	42	67	71	106	177
46	Jan 23	H	Pitt	4-3	W	1	1	2	26	43	69	26	43	69	72	107	179
47	Jan 26	H	Tor	8-3	W	0	2	2	26	45	71	26	45	71	72	109	181
48	Jan 27	H	Phil	5-3	L	1	1	2	27	46	73	27	46	73	73	110	183
49	Jan 29	A	StL	3-2	L	0	0	0	27	46	73	27	46	73	73	110	183
50	Jan 30	A	LA	8-1	W	1	4	5	28	50	78	28	50	78	74	114	188
51	Feb 1	H	Wpg	9-2	W	3	1	4	31	51	82	31	51	82	77	115	192
52	Feb 3	H	LA	5-3	W	1	1	2	32	52	84	32	52	84	78	116	194

Eighteen, Going On Nineteen
Tied for Tops (1979-80) for Openers

No.	Date		H/A	Team	Scr	W/L	Game Totals G	A	Pts	1979-80 Totals G	A	Pts	N.H.L. Career G	A	Pts	Majors (Incl. WHA) G	A	Pts
53	Feb	6	H	StL	6-3	L	1	2	3	33	54	87	33	54	87	79	118	197
54	Feb	8	H	Atl	4-2	L	1	0	1	34	54	88	34	54	88	80	118	198
55	Feb	10	A	Wpg	2-2	T	0	0	0	34	54	88	34	54	88	80	118	198
56	Feb	13	A	Minn	5-3	W	0	1	1	34	55	89	34	55	89	80	119	199
57	Feb	15	H	Wash	8-2	W	0	7	7	34	62	96	34	62	96	80	126	206
58	Feb	17	H	StL	5-5	T	1	2	3	35	64	99	35	64	99	81	128	209
59	Feb	19	A	Hart	6-2	L	0	0	0	35	64	99	35	64	99	81	128	209
60	Feb	20	A	NYR	4-1	L	0	0	0	35	64	99	35	64	99	81	128	209
61	Feb	22	A	Col	3-1	L	0	0	0	35	64	99	35	64	99	81	128	209
62	Feb	24	H	Bos	4-2	L	0	1	1	35	65	100	35	65	100	81	129	210
63	Feb	27	A	Chi	5-2	W	0	2	2	35	67	102	35	67	102	81	131	212
64	Feb	29	H	Buff	4-2	L	0	1	1	35	68	103	35	68	103	81	132	213
65	Mar	1	H	Van	5-2	L	0	0	0	35	68	103	35	68	103	81	132	213
66	Mar	4	A	NYI	6-4	L	2	2	4	37	70	107	37	70	107	83	134	217
67	Mar	6	A	Mtl	5-4	L	1	2	3	38	72	110	38	72	110	84	136	220
68	Mar	8	A	Pitt	5-4	L	1	1	2	39	73	112	39	73	112	85	137	222
69	Mar	9	A	Phil	5-3	L	0	1	1	39	74	113	39	74	113	85	138	223
70	Mar	12	A	Que	6-3	W	2	0	2	41	74	115	41	74	115	87	138	225
71	Mar	14	H	Chi	6-4	W	0	0	0	41	74	115	41	74	115	87	138	225
72	Mar	15	H	Mtl	7-3	L	1	0	1	42	74	116	42	74	116	88	138	226
73	Mar	19	H	NYR	4-2	W	0	1	1	42	75	117	42	75	117	88	139	227
74	Mar	21	H	Pitt	9-2	W	3	1	4	45	76	121	45	76	121	91	140	231
75	Mar	25	A	Atl	5-4	W	2	2	4	47	78	125	47	78	125	93	142	235
76	Mar	26	A	Det	5-2	W	0	2	2	47	80	127	47	80	127	93	144	237
77	Mar	29	A	Tor	8-5	W	2	4	6	49	84	133	49	84	133	95	148	243
78	Apr	1	A	Van	5-0	L	0	0	0	49	84	133	49	84	133	95	148	243
79	Apr	2	H	Minn	1-1	T	1	0	1	50	84	134	50	84	134	96	148	244
80	Apr	4	H	Col	6-2	W	1	2	3	51	86	137	51	86	137	97	150	247

Nineteen, Going On Twenty:
The Year (1980-81) of the Records

No.	Date		H/A	Team	Scr	W/L	Game Totals G	A	Pts	1980-81 Totals G	A	Pts	N.H.L. Career G	A	Pts	Majors (Incl. WHA) G	A	Pts
1	Oct	10	H	Que	7-4	L	2	1	3	2	1	3	53	87	140	99	151	250
2	Oct	13	H	Col	3-2	L	0	2	2	2	3	5	53	89	142	99	153	252
3	Oct	15	A	Buff	2-0	L	0	0	0	2	3	5	53	89	142	99	153	252
4	Oct	18	A	NYI	5-5	T	2	1	3	4	4	8	55	90	145	101	154	255
5	Oct	19	A	NYR	4-2	W	1	3	4	5	7	12	56	93	149	102	157	259
6	Oct	22	H	Cal	5-3	W	0	2	2	5	9	14	56	95	151	102	159	261

Nineteen, Going On Twenty:
The Year (1980-81) of the Records

No.	Date	H/A	Team	Scr	W/L	Game Totals G	Game Totals A	Game Totals Pts	1980-81 Totals G	1980-81 Totals A	1980-81 Totals Pts	N.H.L. Career G	N.H.L. Career A	N.H.L. Career Pts	Majors (Incl. WHA) G	Majors (Incl. WHA) A	Majors (Incl. WHA) Pts
7	Oct 24	H	Minn	4-2	L	0	0	0	5	9	14	56	95	151	102	159	261
8	Oct 26	H	LA	4-4	T	0	0	0	5	9	14	56	95	151	102	159	261
9	Oct 29	H	Tor	4-4	T	0	2	2	5	11	16	56	97	153	102	161	263
10	Nov 1	H	Wash	2-2	T	0	0	0	5	11	16	56	97	153	102	161	263
11	Nov 3	H	Pitt	4-4	T	2	0	2	7	11	18	58	97	155	104	161	265
12	Nov 5	A	Van	4-3	L	0	2	2	7	13	20	58	99	157	104	163	267
13	Nov 7	A	Wpg	4-2	W	0	1	1	7	14	21	58	100	158	104	164	268
14	Nov 9	H	StL	6-4	L	0	2	2	7	16	23	58	102	160	104	166	270
15	Nov 13	A	Phil	8-1	L	0	0	0	7	16	23	58	102	160	104	166	270
16	Nov 15	A	Tor	4-2	L	1	0	1	8	16	24	59	102	161	105	166	271
17	Nov 16	A	Chi	5-4	W	1	2	3	9	18	27	60	104	164	106	168	274
18	Nov 19	H	Van	6-4	L	0	2	2	9	20	29	60	106	166	106	170	276
19	Nov 23	H	Buff	6-3	W	0	1	1	9	21	30	60	107	167	106	171	277
20	Nov 25	A	Col	4-3	L	0	1	1	9	22	31	60	108	168	106	172	278
21	Nov 26	H	Chi	10-3	W	1	4	5	10	26	36	61	112	173	107	176	283
22	Nov 28	A	Hart	6-4	L	0	2	2	10	28	38	61	114	175	107	178	285
23	Nov 29	A	Bos	6-3	L	1	0	1	11	28	39	62	114	176	108	178	286
24	Dec 5	H	NYR	5-1	L	1	0	1	12	28	40	63	114	177	109	178	287
25	Dec 7	H	Hart	6-4	W	1	2	3	13	30	43	64	116	180	110	180	290
26	Dec 10	H	NYI	3-2	L	0	0	0	13	30	43	64	116	180	110	180	290
27	Dec 13	A	Mtl	4-1	L	0	1	1	13	31	44	64	117	181	110	181	291
28	Dec 14	A	Que	6-5	L	0	1	1	13	32	45	64	118	182	110	182	292
29	Dec 16	A	Det	4-3	L	0	2	2	13	34	47	64	120	184	110	184	294
30	Dec 17	A	Wash	5-2	L	0	0	0	13	34	47	64	120	184	110	184	294
31	Dec 20	H	Mtl	4-3	W	0	1	1	13	35	48	64	121	185	110	185	295
32	Dec 23	A	LA	7-4	L	3	0	3	16	35	51	67	121	188	113	185	298
33	Dec 27	H	Det	4-4	T	0	3	3	16	38	54	67	124	191	113	188	301
34	Dec 28	H	Phil	2-1	L	0	0	0	16	38	54	67	124	191	113	188	301
35	Dec 30	A	Cal	5-3	L	1	1	2	17	39	56	68	125	193	114	189	303
36	Jan 2	H	Bos	7-5	W	0	1	1	17	40	57	68	126	194	114	190	304
37	Jan 3	H	Tor	4-1	W	1	2	3	18	42	60	69	128	197	115	192	307
38	Jan 7	H	Wash	6-3	W	2	2	4	20	44	64	71	130	201	117	194	311
39	Jan 9	H	Hart	6-6	T	0	1	1	20	45	65	71	131	202	117	195	312
40	Jan 11	A	Que	6-3	W	1	4	5	21	49	70	72	135	207	118	199	317
41	Jan 12	A	Mtl	5-0	L	0	0	0	21	49	70	72	135	207	118	199	317
42	Jan 14	A	Tor	7-4	W	2	1	3	23	50	73	74	136	210	120	200	320
43	Jan 16	A	Buff	5-5	T	0	0	0	23	50	73	74	136	210	120	200	320
44	Jan 17	A	StL	7-6	L	1	3	4	24	53	77	75	139	214	121	203	324
45	Jan 21	H	Van	5-1	W	1	2	3	25	55	80	76	141	217	122	205	327
46	Jan 23	H	NYR	7-4	L	0	2	2	25	57	82	76	143	219	122	207	329
47	Jan 24	A	Minn	6-1	L	0	1	1	25	58	83	76	144	220	122	208	330
48	Jan 28	H	Mtl	9-1	W	1	4	5	26	62	88	77	148	225	123	212	335
49	Jan 30	H	Chi	4-2	W	1	2	3	27	64	91	78	150	228	124	214	338

Nineteen, Going On Twenty: The Year (1980-81) of the Records

No.	Date	H/A	Team	Scr	W/L	Game Totals G	A	Pts	1980-81 Totals G	A	Pts	N.H.L. Career G	A	Pts	Majors (Incl. WHA) G	A	Pts
50	Feb 1	A	Wash	7-4	L	0	2	2	27	66	93	78	152	230	124	216	340
51	Feb 3	A	StL	3-3	T	0	0	0	27	66	93	78	152	230	124	216	340
52	Feb 4	A	Chi	6-3	L	1	0	1	28	66	94	79	152	231	125	216	341
53	Feb 6	H	Wpg	10-4	W	3	3	6	31	69	100	82	155	237	128	219	347
54	Feb 8	H	Cal	10-4	L	1	2	3	32	71	103	83	157	240	129	221	350
55	Feb 13	H	Que	4-2	L	1	0	1	33	71	104	84	157	241	130	221	351
56	Feb 14	H	Buff	2-2	T	0	1	1	33	72	105	84	158	242	130	222	352
57	Feb 17	H	StL	9-2	W	5	2	7	38	74	112	89	160	249	135	224	359
58	Feb 19	H	Bos	5-1	L	0	0	0	38	74	112	89	160	249	135	224	359
59	Feb 21	H	Wpg	5-1	W	0	1	1	38	75	113	89	161	250	135	225	360
60	Feb 24	A	LA	5-2	L	1	0	1	39	75	114	90	161	251	136	225	361
61	Feb 25	H	Phil	6-2	W	2	2	4	41	77	118	92	163	255	138	227	365
62	Feb 27	H	Det	5-2	W	1	1	2	42	78	120	93	164	257	139	228	367
63	Feb 28	A	Col	3-1	L	0	1	1	42	79	121	93	165	258	139	229	368
64	Mar 3	A	NYI	8-8	T	2	2	4	44	81	125	95	167	262	141	231	372
65	Mar 4	A	NYR	5-5	T	1	0	1	45	81	126	96	167	263	142	231	373
66	Mar 7	A	Phil	5-3	W	4	0	4	49	81	130	100	167	267	146	231	377
67	Mar 8	A	Pitt	6-4	L	0	1	1	49	82	131	100	168	268	146	232	378
68	Mar 12	H	NYI	5 0	L	0	0	0	49	82	131	100	168	268	146	232	378
69	Mar 15	A	Cal	3-3	T	1	0	1	50	82	132	101	168	269	147	232	379
70	Mar 16	H	Pitt	7-6	W	0	3	3	50	85	135	101	171	272	147	235	382
71	Mar 18	A	Minn	5-3	W	0	4	4	50	89	139	101	175	276	147	239	386
72	Mar 20	H	Minn	1-1	T	1	0	1	51	89	140	102	175	277	148	239	387
73	Mar 21	H	LA	6-6	T	1	4	5	52	93	145	103	179	282	149	243	392
74	Mar 23	A	Bos	7-2	W	0	2	2	52	95	147	103	181	284	149	245	394
75	Mar 25	A	Hart	7-2	W	1	3	4	53	98	151	104	184	288	150	248	398
76	Mar 28	A	Det	4-2	W	0	1	1	53	99	152	104	185	289	150	249	399
77	Mar 29	A	Pitt	5-2	W	0	3	3	53	102	155	104	188	292	150	252	402
78	Apr 1	H	Col	4-4	T	0	2	2	53	104	157	104	190	294	150	254	404
79	Apr 3	A	Van	7-2	W	1	1	2	54	105	159	105	191	296	151	255	406
80	Apr 4	H	Wpg	7-2	W	1	4	5	55	109	164	106	195	301	152	259	411

Twenty, Going On Twenty-One
The Greatest Single Season (1981-82)

No	Date	H/A	Team	Scr	W/L	Game Totals G	A	Pts	1981-82 Season G	A	Pts	N.H.L. Career G	A	Pts	Majors (Incl. WHA) G	A	Pts
1	Oct 7	H	Col	7-4	W	0	1	1	0	1	1	106	196	302	152	260	412
2	Oct 9	A	Van	6-2	L	0	0	0	0	1	1	106	196	302	152	260	412
3	Oct 10	A	LA	7-4	W	1	1	2	1	2	3	107	197	304	153	261	414
4	Oct 14	H	Wpg	4-2	L	1	0	1	2	2	4	108	197	305	154	261	415

Twenty, Going On Twenty-One
The Greatest Single Season (1981-82)

No	Date	H/A	Team	Scr	W/L	Game Totals G	A	Pts	1981-82 Season G	A	Pts	N.H.L. Career G	A	Pts	Majors (Incl. WHA) G	A	Pts
5	Oct 16	H	Cal	8-4	W	1	2	3	3	4	7	109	199	308	155	263	418
6	Oct 18	A	Chi	7-5	L	1	3	4	4	7	11	110	202	312	156	266	422
7	Oct 20	A	Cal	5-4	W	1	1	2	5	8	13	111	203	314	157	267	424
8	Oct 21	H	Hart	5-2	W	0	0	0	5	8	13	111	203	314	157	267	424
9	Oct 23	H	Pitt	8-3	W	1	2	3	6	10	16	112	205	317	158	269	427
10	Oct 24	A	Col	3-1	W	1	0	1	7	10	17	113	205	318	159	269	428
11	Oct 27	A	NYI	4-3	L	0	1	1	7	11	18	113	206	319	159	270	429
12	Oct 28	A	NYR	5-3	W	2	2	4	9	13	22	115	208	323	161	272	433
13	Oct 31	H	Que	11-4	W	4	1	5	13	14	27	119	209	328	165	273	438
14	Nov 4	H	Tor	6-4	W	2	0	2	15	14	29	121	209	330	167	273	440
15	Nov 7	H	Col	5-4	L	0	0	0	15	14	29	121	209	330	167	273	440
16	Nov 11	A	Hart	4-4	T	2	1	3	17	15	32	123	210	333	169	274	443
17	Nov 12	A	Bos	5-2	L	0	2	2	17	17	34	123	212	335	169	276	445
18	Nov 14	A	NYI	5-5	T	1	3	4	18	20	38	124	215	339	170	279	449
19	Nov 15	A	NYR	5-3	W	1	2	3	19	22	41	125	217	342	171	281	452
20	Nov 17	A	StL	5-1	W	2	1	3	21	23	44	127	218	345	173	282	455
21	Nov 19	A	Minn	2-2	T	0	0	0	21	23	44	127	218	345	173	282	455
22	Nov 21	H	Van	8-3	W	2	2	4	23	25	48	129	220	349	175	284	459
23	Nov 23	H	Det	8-4	W	1	1	2	24	26	50	130	221	351	176	285	461
24	Nov 25	H	LA	11-4	W	4	1	5	28	27	55	134	222	356	180	286	466
25	Nov 27	H	Chi	8-1	W	2	3	5	30	30	60	136	225	361	182	289	471
26	Nov 29	A	Wpg	10-2	W	1	3	4	31	33	64	137	228	365	183	292	475
27	Dec 1	A	Mtl	3-3	T	0	3	3	31	36	67	137	231	368	183	295	478
28	Dec 2	A	Que	9-8	L	0	2	2	31	38	69	137	233	370	183	297	481
29	Dec 4	H	Van	7-3	W	0	3	3	31	41	72	137	236	373	183	300	483
30	Dec 5	A	Van	3-3	T	0	2	2	31	43	74	137	238	375	183	302	485
31	Dec 9	A	LA	5-5	T	1	0	1	32	43	75	138	238	376	184	302	486
32	Dec 13	H	NYI	4-3	W	1	3	4	33	46	79	139	241	380	185	305	490
33	Dec 16	A	Col	7-4	W	1	2	3	34	48	82	140	243	383	186	307	493
34	Dec 17	A	Cal	5-4	W	1	0	1	35	48	83	141	243	384	187	307	494
35	Dec 19	H	Minn	9-6	W	3	4	7	38	52	90	144	247	391	190	311	501
36	Dec 20	H	Cal	7-5	L	2	1	3	40	53	93	146	248	394	192	312	504
37	Dec 23	H	Van	6-1	W	1	3	4	41	56	97	147	251	398	193	315	508
38	Dec 27	H	LA	10-3	W	4	1	5	45	57	102	151	252	403	197	316	513
39	Dec 30	H	Phil	7-5	W	5	1	6	50	58	108	156	253	409	202	317	519
40	Dec 31	A	Van	3-1	L	0	0	0	50	58	108	156	253	409	202	317	519
41	Jan 2	H	Bos	4-4	T	1	1	2	51	59	110	157	254	411	203	318	521
42	Jan 6	H	Col	5-3	W	2	2	4	53	61	114	159	256	415	205	320	525
43	Jan 9	H	Cal	7-2	W	1	4	5	54	65	119	160	260	420	206	324	530
44	Jan 10	A	Cal	5-1	L	0	0	0	54	65	119	160	260	420	206	324	530
45	Jan 13	A	Wash	6-6	T	1	2	3	55	67	122	161	262	423	207	326	533
46	Jan 14	A	Phil	8-2	L	1	0	1	56	67	123	162	262	424	208	326	534
47	Jan 16	A	Tor	7-1	L	1	0	1	57	67	124	163	262	425	209	326	535

Twenty, Going On Twenty-One
The Greatest Single Season (1981-82)

No	Date	H/A	Team	Scr	W/L	Game Totals			1981-82 Season			N.H.L. Career			Majors (Incl. WHA)		
						G	A	Pts	G	A	Pts	G	A	Pts	G	A	Pts
48	Jan 17	A	Det	4-4	T	0	2	2	57	69	126	163	264	427	209	328	537
49	Jan 20	H	St.L	8-6	W	3	2	5	60	71	131	166	266	432	212	330	542
50	Jan 22	A	Van	4-3	W	1	1	2	61	72	133	167	267	434	213	331	544
51	Jan 24	H	Col	7-4	W	0	3	3	61	75	136	167	270	437	213	334	547
52	Jan 26	A	St.L	6-4	W	1	1	2	62	76	138	168	271	439	214	335	549
53	Jan 27	A	Chic	3-3	T	1	1	2	63	77	140	169	272	441	215	336	551
54	Jan 29	H	Buff	3-1	W	1	0	1	64	77	141	170	272	442	216	336	552
55	Jan 31	H	Phil	7-4	W	3	2	5	67	79	146	173	274	447	219	338	557
56	Feb 3	H	Mtl	6-3	L	1	1	2	68	80	148	174	275	449	220	339	559
57	Feb 6	H	Tor	5-1	W	0	2	2	68	82	150	174	277	451	220	341	561
58	Feb 7	H	NYR	8-4	W	1	1	2	69	83	152	175	278	453	221	342	563
59	Feb 12	H	Wash	5-3	W	1	2	3	70	85	155	176	280	456	222	344	566
60	Feb 14	H	Bos	2-2	T	0	1	1	70	86	156	176	281	457	222	345	567
61	Feb 17	H	Minn	7-4	W	2	3	5	72	89	161	178	284	462	224	348	572
62	Feb 19	H	Hart	7-4	W	3	2	5	75	91	166	181	286	467	227	350	577
63	Feb 21	A	Det	7-3	W	1	4	5	76	95	171	182	290	472	228	354	582
64	Feb 24	A	Buff	6-3	W	3	2	5	79	97	176	185	292	477	231	356	587
65	Feb 27	A	Pitt	4-1	W	1	1	2	80	98	178	186	293	479	232	357	589
66	Feb 28	A	Wash	4-1	W	2	1	3	82	99	181	188	294	482	234	358	592
67	Mar 2	A	Mtl	3-3	T	0	2	2	82	101	183	188	296	484	234	360	594
68	Mar 3	A	Que	6-4	L	0	2	2	82	103	185	188	298	486	234	362	596
69	Mar 6	A	Col	5-2	L	0	0	0	82	103	185	188	298	486	234	362	596
70	Mar 10	A	LA	3-2	L	0	2	2	82	105	187	188	300	488	234	364	598
71	Mar 12	H	Buff	3-2	L	0	0	0	82	105	187	188	300	488	234	364	598
72	Mar 13	H	Van	5-3	W	0	3	3	82	108	190	188	303	491	234	367	601
73	Mar 15	H	LA	3-3	T	2	0	2	84	108	192	190	303	493	236	369	603
74	Mar 17	H	Pitt	10-4	W	3	2	5	87	110	197	193	305	498	239	371	608
75	Mar 19	H	Cal	3-3	T	1	1	2	88	111	199	194	306	500	240	372	610
76	Mar 25	A	Cal	7-2	W	2	2	4	90	113	203	196	308	504	242	374	614
77	Mar 26	A	Col	6-6	T	1	2	3	91	115	206	197	310	507	243	376	617
78	Mar 28	A	LA	6-2	W	1	1	2	92	116	208	198	311	509	244	377	619
79	Mar 31	H	LA	7-3	W	0	3	3	92	119	211	198	314	512	244	380	622
80	Apr 4	H	Wpg	2-1	W	0	1	1	92	120	212	198	315	513	244	381	623

Twenty-One, Going On Twenty-Two:
The Season (1982-83) at Hand

No.	Date	H/A	Team	Scr	W/L	Game Totals			1982-83 Totals			N.H.L. Career			Majors (Incl. WHA)		
						G	A	Pts	G	A	Pts	G	A	Pts	G	A	Pts
1	Oct 5	H	Cal														
2	Oct 8	H	NYI														
3	Oct 9	A	Van														
4	Oct 12	A	Cal														

Twenty-One, Going On Twenty-Two:
The Season (1982-83) at Hand

No. Date	H/A	Team	Scr	W/L	Game Totals			1982-83 Totals			N.H.L. Career			Majors (Incl. WHA)		
					G	A	Pts	G	A	Pts	G	A	Pts	G	A	Pts
5 Oct 14	A	Hart														
6 Oct 16	A	Bos														
7 Oct 17	A	Buff														
8 Oct 20	H	Hart														
9 Oct 21	H	Bos														
10 Oct 24	A	Wpg														
11 Oct 27	H	Chic														
12 Oct 29	H	LA														
13 Oct 31	H	Van														
14 Nov 3	H	Wpg														
15 Nov 5	H	NYR														
16 Nov 8	A	Que														
17 Nov 10	A	Pitt														
18 Nov 11	A	NJ														
19 Nov 13	A	Phil														
20 Nov 14	A	NYR														
21 Nov 16	A	NYI														
22 Nov 20	H	Van														
23 Nov 21	H	Que														
24 Nov 24	H	Wash														
25 Nov 26	A	Wpg														
26 Nov 28	A	Det														
27 Dec 1	H	Phil														
28 Dec 4	H	Cal														
29 Dec 5	H	LA														
30 Dec 7	H	St.L														
31 Dec 9	A	LA														
32 Dec 11	A	Minn														
33 Dec 17	H	NJ														
34 Dec 19	H	Mtl														
35 Dec 22	H	Minn														
36 Dec 23	A	LA														
37 Dec 26	A	Cal														
38 Dec 29	H	Chic														
39 Dec 31	A	Van														
40 Jan 1	H	Wpg														
41 Jan 4	A	Cal														
42 Jan 5	A	Wpg														

Twenty-One, Going On Twenty-Two: The Season (1982-83) at Hand

No.	Date	H/A	Team	Scr	W/L	Game Totals			1982-83 Totals			N.H.L. Career			Majors (Incl. WHA)		
						G	A	Pts	G	A	Pts	G	A	Pts	G	A	Pts
43	Jan 7	H	Pitt	___	___												
44	Jan 9	H	Det	___	___												
45	Jan 11	A	St.L	___	___												
46	Jan 12	A	Chic	___	___												
47	Jan 15	A	Minn	___	___												
48	Jan 18	A	LA	___	___												
49	Jan 19	H	Van	___	___												
50	Jan 22	A	Van	___	___												
51	Jan 23	H	LA	___	___												
52	Jan 26	H	Tor	___	___												

(Wayne Gretzky's 22nd Birthday)

No.	Date	H/A	Team	Scr	W/L	G	A	Pts	G	A	Pts	G	A	Pts	G	A	Pts
53	Jan 29	H	Cal	___	___												
54	Jan 30	H	NYI	___	___												
55	Feb 3	H	LA	___	___												
56	Feb 4	H	Mtl	___	___												
57	Feb 11	H	Que	___	___												
58	Feb 14	A	Mtl	___	___												
59	Feb 17	A	Phil	___	___												
60	Feb 19	A	Pitt	___	___												
61	Feb 20	A	Buff	___	___												
62	Feb 22	A	Cal	___	___												
63	Feb 23	H	Wash	___	___												
64	Feb 25	H	St.L	___	___												
65	Feb 27	H	Wpg	___	___												
66	Mar 1	A	NJ	___	___												
67	Mar 2	A	Wash	___	___												
68	Mar 5	A	Tor	___	___												
69	Mar 6	A	Bos	___	___												
70	Mar 8	A	Hart	___	___												
71	Mar 11	H	NYR	___	___												
72	Mar 13	H	Buff	___	___												
73	Mar 16	H	Van	___	___												
74	Mar 19	H	Pitt	___	___												
75	Mar 21	A	Tor	___	___												
76	Mar 23	A	Wpg	___	___												
77	Mar 26	A	LA	___	___												
78	Mar 29	A	Van	___	___												
79	Apr 1	H	Wpg	___	___												
80	Apr 3	H	Cal	___	___												